Introduction –

Ocean City High School graduated its first class in 1904, from a building on Central Avenue near Ninth Street. There were six students in the first graduating class. In 1924, a new building was constructed on the block between Fifth and Sixth Streets and between Atlantic and Ocean Avenues. That building was expanded in 1963. The school fielded sports teams almost from the beginning, though the original colors were blue and white, later to be changed to red and white.

The Cape-Atlantic League (CAL) was formed in the fall of 1948 by six schools – Cape May, Egg Harbor City, Hammonton, Middle Township (in Cape May Court House), Ocean City and Wildwood. In 1960, Egg Harbor City closed its doors and Oakcrest opened in Mays Landing. The next year – 1961-62 – Mainland Regional opened and joined the league, together with Pleasantville. And, in 1968-69, Sacred Heart and Wildwood Catholic became the first non-public schools to join.

Though Ocean City High School dates back into the early years of the 20th Century, for the purposes of high school sports it is foolish to consider anything that happened prior to 1918 when the New Jersey State Interscholastic Athletic Association (NJSIAA) was formed. Prior to that, there were no rules governing high school sports and teams frequently included alumni, faculty members and even soldiers home on leave.

In the chapters that follow, we review each school year that concludes with a graduation during the 1960s. There is also a summary of some of the highlights of the seasons prior to 1960. These reviews include the scores, stats, stories and photos of the athletes and coaches who helped build the record of success that the Raiders have enjoyed from the very beginning.

Ken Leary, Don Tarves, Fenton Carey, Dixie Howell, John Cranston, John Henry, Ed McClain, Earl Tarves, John Huff, John Cervino, Bill Haynes, Ken Penska….these are just a few of the names that made the 1960s an important decade in the history of Ocean City High School sports.

Photos in this book are from the files of Bill Gaskill, Tom Williams and Caravel, the Ocean City High School yearbook. They are used with permission.

We expect to follow this book with others devoted to later decades but, in this initial publication, we hope you will enjoy reviewing the great successes, the tragedies and the challenges that Ocean City High School's student-athletes experienced in the 1960s, and before.

Chapter One

1959-60

The school year 1959-60 was the beginning of an exciting decade. Things would change in music, in politics, in film, on television and in sports.

In October, Rod Serling's "The Twilight Zone", destined to become a TV classic, debuted on CBS. In January, Massachusetts Senator John F. Kennedy announced his candidacy for President of the United States. In February, the very first star on the Hollywood Walk of Fame was awarded to Joanne Woodward. In March, Sgt. Elvis Presley received his honorable discharge from the U.S. Army. In April, the first weather satellite was launched. And in May, President Dwight Eisenhower signed the Civil Rights Act of 1960.

"Ben-Hur" won the 1960 Oscar as best picture. The record of the year was "Mack the Knife" by Bobby Darin. The best actor on TV was Robert Stack in "The Untouchables". The Dodgers beat the White Sox in the 1959 World Series. In pro football, the Baltimore Colts won the NFL championship by beating the New York Giants. Ohio State defeated California to win the NCAA basketball title. The Boston Celtics were the NBA champions, beating the St. Louis Hawks in seven games. And Cassius Clay (later to change his name to Muhammad Ali) won the Olympic boxing gold medal at the XVII games in Rome.

There were five varsity sports teams at Ocean City High School, all for boys. Football played in the fall on the Recreation Center Field (now Carey Stadium) off the Boardwalk at Sixth Street. In the winter there was basketball and swimming, with a small pool in the high school building between Atlantic and Ocean Avenues. And the spring brought baseball and track, conducted at facilities between Fifth and Sixth Streets – one near the ocean and the other across the street from the bay.

Fred Haack's football team finished 6-3 despite losing its opener, 26-18, to Toms River High School. What followed were five straight wins over Woodstown (6-0), Wildwood (9-0), Cape May

(21-6), Hammonton (7-6) and Egg Harbor City (31-6). The streak was ended when Millville beat them, 19-0. The Raiders had a chance to win the Cape-Atlantic League but lost to Middle Township, 9-6, and the Panthers became league champions. Ocean City shut out Pleasantville, 19-0, on Thanksgiving.

The OCHS offense was built around the "T-D" combination of "Tarves-Davis". Don Tarves averaged 9.8 yards per carry over the course of the season and gained 1,085 rushing yards. The duo was one of the most effective offensive combinations in South Jersey. They graduated having gained close to 2,000 yards between them.

The basketball team was undefeated Cape-Atlantic League champions, finishing the season with 45 straight wins against CAL opponents over six seasons. Dixie Howell's Raiders were 19-2 and lost only to St. Joseph's of Camden in the South Jersey Christmas Tournament and to Burlington City in the first round of the NJSIAA Group 3 Tournament.

Ocean City won a series of impressive non-league victories over Millville, Bishop Eustace, Clayton, Pleasantville, Vineland, Woodbury and Holy Spirit. They finished with an average of 77.8 points per game, a new school record for one season. They also scored 111 points against Egg Harbor City to set a new school record for a single game.

Four players finished with double-figure scoring averages. Ken Leary led the way with 16.4 per game, Gary Satrappe added 16.3, Jim Bernosky 14.7 and Warner Christy 10.6. It marked the first season in school history when Ocean City had four players average scoring in double figures. The Raiders also got 8.7 points a game from Butch Krattenmaker, who made an impressive 74 percent of his free throws. In fact, the Raiders shot over 66 percent as a team from the line.

In the Raiders second win against Pleasantville, Leary became the first player in OCHS history to record a triple-double. He finished the game with 19 points, 10 rebounds and 11 steals. In addition, the 11 steals in one game was a school record. Ironically, Leary would later coach Pleasantville to 519 wins, eight South Jersey titles and three state titles. Leary also became the third player in school history to score 40 or more in a game when he scored 40 points against Middle Township. Mike Fadden (48) and Wayne Thompson (40) did it before him.

The swim team finished with a 6-3 record, including wins over Malvern Prep (57-29), Valley Forge Military Academy (48-38) and Moorestown (52-34). Seniors Jack Davis and Don Tarves made the quick transition from football to lead the Raiders in the pool. Tarves' strength was in freestyle events while Davis was most effective off the diving board. Seniors Bob Adams and Otto Fernsel were also key parts of the lineup.

But this swim team was loaded with young athletes who would make even bigger impressions in subsequent seasons. That group included Bruce Presti, Hank Schneider, John Stull, Harry Smith, Norman Ervine, Mike Hamilton and Fenton Carey Jr.

The baseball team, coached by Dixie Howell and hoping to defend its CAL championship, opened with a 7-1 win over Wildwood. Orville Mathis pitched a five-hitter. Don Tarves and

Jim Bernosky each had a double and two singles. The Raiders lost to Egg Harbor City, 2-0, despite the two-hit pitching of Cliff Lilley. Tarves and Lynn Baker each had two singles. They also lost to Hammonton, 4-3, with Mathis driving home two runs.

After an 8-4 non-league loss to George (PA) School, the Raiders defeated Middle Township, 14-2. OCHS scored 10 times in the second inning with Baker getting a three-run triple and Tarves a two-run single. They then defeated Wildwood, 3-0, on Lilley's four-hitter. Mathis had three hits and Baker added two. Ocean City also defeated Lower Cape May, 12-8. Mathis had two triples and two singles and Fred Boyce had three singles. Bob Spence was the winning pitcher in relief.

Lilley pitched a no-hitter against Holy Spirit and got the win by driving home Boyce with the game's only run himself. Mathis had pitched a no-hitter earlier in the season but lost the game.

Millville defeated the Raiders in the NJSIAA Group 3 Tournament, 6-2. Ocean City finished second to Wildwood in the final CAL standings, despite beating the Warriors twice.

Fenton Carey's track team defeated Middle Township, 75-24. Len Migliaccio was a double winner, taking the javelin and broad jump. Other winners were John Stull (880 yard run), Rich Buggelin (mile), Craig Moncrief (high jump), Tom DeBaufre (shot put) and Bob Adams (discus).

The Raiders won the CAL Championship Meet with Jack Davis winning both the 440 and the broad jump. Other winners in the CAL Meet were Buggelin in the mile, Marty Petrusky in the 880 and Don Tarves, who traded his baseball uniform for track spikes and won the CAL high jump.

Ocean City also defeated Pleasantville, 68-31, with Davis winning three events. They topped Wildwood, 73-26, despite a double win by the Warriors' Randy Beverly, a future Super Bowl hero for the New York Jets. And they beat Cape May, 77-22, with Migliaccio winning twice and just missing a triple.

Chapter Two

1960-61

Excitement continued in the 1960-61 school year. And 1961 was also the first year since 1881 where the numerals could be turned upside down and still read the same. It won't happen again until 6009.

Early in the school year, Ocean City High School students were shocked into mourning when Bruce Presti, a senior and co-captain of the Raiders swim team, was killed in an auto accident in Tuckahoe. During the summer, Presti had made news when he was one of a small group of lifeguards who rescued a swimmer who was attacked by a shark off the Sixth Street beach.

In January, Mickey Mantle signed a $75,000 contract with the New York Yankees, making him baseball's highest paid player. A few days later, John F. Kennedy took the oath as the youngest President of the United States and Ocean City's Phil Turner directed the decoration at some of the Inaugural Balls. In February, the Beatles performed for the first time in Liverpool. In March, the city's new advertising agency decided to stop using "America's Greatest Family Resort" as a slogan because it was "too boastful". That idea barely lasted through the summer. And. in May, Ocean City residents began using dial telephones and the phone exchange of Export 9 became 399.

"The Apartment" won the 1961 Oscar as best picture. The record of the year was "Theme from a Summer Place" by Percy Faith. The best actor on TV was Raymond Burr in "Perry Mason". The Pirates beat the Yankees in the 1960 World Series on Bill Mazeroski's walk-off home run in game seven. In pro football, the Philadelphia Eagles won the NFL championship by beating the Packers. Cincinnati defeated Ohio State to win the NCAA basketball title and Jack Ramsay's St. Joseph's Hawks reached the Final Four. The Boston Celtics were the NBA champions. And a chubby blonde from Ohio State named Jack Nicklaus was the U.S. Amateur Golf Champion.

Things were going to change at Ocean City High School. The 1960-61 school year was to be the final time that students from Somers Point and Linwood would come to OCHS. A new high school would open in Linwood in September of 1961.

The football team, coached by Fred Haack, started the season with four straight losses, scoring only twice in the four games. This was Haack's third and final season as head coach. His teams had been 11-6-1 the first two seasons. The Raiders earned their first victory, 32-0, over Hammonton. Quarterback Coke Hall threw two TD passes – one to Dick Fox and one to John Stull. The other TDs came on the ground from Harry Smith, Bill Gleeson and Dan Henry. Smith's score was a 90-yard run.

The Raiders made it two straight the following week when Dan Weeks scooped up a fumble and ran 70 yards for the game's only score in a 6-0 win over Oakcrest. The Mays Landing school had just opened, taking students largely from Egg Harbor City High School, which had closed in June.

Ocean City then lost to Millville before tying Middle Township, 13-13, and defeating Pleasantville, 13-6. Hall and Henry scored the two TDs and Cliff Lilley kicked an extra point to give OCHS a 13-0 lead over Middle. The Raiders then had to hold off the Panthers' second half rally. On Thanksgiving morning, Hall threw TDs to Fox and Fred Boyce to win the rivalry game.

The basketball team, coached by Dixie Howell, started the season with four straight wins. The team split with Wildwood in the Cape-Atlantic League and won the championship when Wildwood suffered an upset loss to Cape May. When Wildwood beat them, 58-57, the first time around it ended the OCHS win streak against CAL opponents at 47. The Raiders lost non-league games to Neptune, Holy Spirit and Bishop Eustace and won their Christmas Jamboree, the one-night tournament where teams played half games.

During the course of the season, senior co-captain Ken Leary became the first player at a CAL school to score 1,000 career points. Leary reached his milestone with a 29-point effort against Middle Township in a win that clinched the league title for the seventh straight season. He also set school records for steals and assists. And junior Gary Satrappe, a Somers Point resident who would play for Mainland Regional his senior year and lead South Jersey in scoring, became just the second player in OCHS history to average over 20 points per game for a season. His 20.1 average was second to the 20.3 by Mike Fadden three years earlier.

Satrappe ended up as the leading scorer in the CAL with Leary finishing second. Satrappe made 80.6 percent of his free throws and co-captain Butch Krattenmaker made 75.8 percent. Leary, Satrappe and Krattenmaker were joined in the starting lineup by Brad Wickes and a rotating group that included Dick Fox, Jesse Moore and Jerry Fadden.

This team qualified for the New Jersey State Interscholastic Athletic Association's Group 3 Tournament and was beaten by Merchantville in the first round. Leary was awarded the Wilbur Clark Memorial Trophy as the team's most valuable player, selected by his teammates. Leary and Krattenmaker graduated with a combined 1,709 career points, the most by any two players from the same graduating class, breaking the record held by Joe Kennedy and Frank Wickes.

Fenton Carey's swim team had a 9-3 record, led by John Stull and Ron Van Sant (above). The team won the Bruce Presti Memorial Award, named for the OCHS senior who had died in the October automobile accident. It was given to the team between Atlantic City and Ocean City High Schools that scored the most points in the two meets in which they faced each other.

In the pool, the Raiders finished third in the South Jersey Invitational Meet and were sixth in the NJSIAA championship meet. In addition to Stull and Van Sant, successful swimmers included Harry Smith, Hank Schneider, Mike Hamilton, Fred Klein, Norm Ervine, Frank Jankowski, Kjold Christensen, Bruce Smith and Fenton Carey Jr. OCHS faced teams from all over the state during their regular schedule because the CAL had not yet included swimming as a championship sport.

Ervine finished third in the NJSIAA meet, breaking his own record in the butterfly. Carey was sixth in the individual medley in that state meet.

During the spring of 1961, Ocean City's baseball team reached the NJSIAA South Jersey Group 3 championship game. Six teams qualified for the tournament. The Raiders received a bye in the first round and defeated Triton, 5-2, in the semifinals. OCHS was shut out by Audubon, 5-0, in the championship game.

The Raiders, who had a seven-game win streak during the season and won the CAL title for the fourth time in five years, scored three runs in the first inning against Triton. Bill Gemmell and Butch Krattenmaker singled. Gemmell scored on a single by Bob Spence and both Krattenmaker and Spence were driven home on a hit by Cliff Lilley. Later, Fred Boyce was driven in by Charles Mumford, who scored on a hit by Krattenmaker. Lilley was the winning pitcher, shutting out Triton over the final six innings.

Ocean City's track and field team had a good season. The Raiders, coached by Fenton Carey, finished second in the CAL. The Raiders have now finished either first or second in the league for nine straight seasons. Among the strongest competitors for OCHS were Wickes and Bill Brown in the 880 yard run, Rennie Gans in the mile, Craig Moncrief in the high jump, Len Migliaccio in the 220, Harry Lee in the pole vault and Stull in the shot put.

Chapter Three

1961-62

The year 1961-62 was one of change.

In September, Mainland Regional High School opened in Linwood, bringing together students from three communities – Somers Point, Linwood and Northfield. Those from Somers Point and Linwood had previously attended Ocean City High School and those from Northfield had gone to Pleasantville. Mainland became a member of the Cape-Atlantic League and Pleasantville also joined the league.

In October, Roger Maris hit his 61st home run, breaking Babe Ruth's single-season record in major league baseball.

"West Side Story" won the 1962 Oscar as best picture. The record of the year was "Moon River" by Henry Mancini. The best actress on TV was Shirley Booth in "Hazel". The Yankees beat the Reds in a five-game World Series. In pro football, the Packers beat the Giants for the NFL championship. Cincinnati beat Ohio State for the second straight year to win the NCAA title. The Celtics topped the Lakers to win the NBA championship. And Arnold Palmer won the Master's and the British Open.

At Ocean City High School there were still the same five varsity sports teams, all for boys. The Raiders had to replace some athletes who left to attend Mainland. Seniors were given the option to finish at OCHS but most chose to switch to the brand new school off Route 9 in Linwood.

The football team, coached by Andy Prohaska, got off to a bad start, losing its first four games. Prohaska had been an assistant to Fred Haack the previous two seasons but they switched places in 1961 with Haack returning as an assistant. Seniors Harry Smith, Jack Hollingshead, Howard Turner and Harry Bakley and juniors John Burch and Jack Bello were key players.

After the four losses, the Raiders won back-to-back, beating Hammonton, 23-0, with Al McNellis scoring twice, and edging Oakcrest, 14-13, when Jack Hollingshead ran for one TD and Burch (above) hit McNellis for the other. Burch ran for one extra point and threw to Bob Townsend for the game-winner.

OCHS then lost a thriller to Mainland, 7-0, when the Mustangs' George Emmons scored the game's lone touchdown in the second quarter. McNellis, one of the few athletes from the mainland communities who elected to remain at OCHS for his senior year, was injured on the opening kickoff and unable to return. Ocean City completed the season with losses to Middle Township and Pleasantville to finish 2-7. Center Harry Bakley was a first team, CAL all star.

Fenton Carey's 1961-62 swim team, captained by Mike Hamilton and Hank Schneider, finished an impressive 12-1 and won the South Jersey championship. The 200 yard freestyle relay team of Harry Smith, Jim Simms, Fred Klein and Hamilton won the state championship and was selected as part of the OCHS

All-Century Swim Team. Hamilton was also named to the All-Century Team for both the 50 and 100 freestyle.

Dixie Howell coached the baseball team to a 9-6 record, led by Charley Mumford's .460 batting average. He had eight extra base hits and nine RBIs in his 50 plate appearances and was 7-3 on the mound with a 2.67 ERA, including a couple of one-hitters and one game where he struck out 16. Jim Wimberg and Frank Petrella both hit .286.

In track, Fenton Carey's team was led by Jerry Fadden, who also captained the basketball team. Fadden was successful in the 100 yard dash and the broad jump. Dan Money was also a strong broad jumper, taking third in the South Jersey Group 2 Meet. Bryan Sherby ran the 220 for the Raiders, Tom Herrington the 880, Fenton Carey Jr. and Rennie Gans ran the mile, Ray Healy threw the discus and Norm Ervine was the pole vaulter.

A new event - the Cape-Atlantic League Relays – was created in the spring of 1962 and OCHS finished second to Lower Cape May, which had also won the league title.

But the big story of 1961-62 was the basketball team and how it was affected by an incredible storm in March, a storm that did $5.5 million in damage (and that's in 1962 money) to Ocean City. The Raiders had won seven straight Cape-Atlantic League championships under Dixie Howell. But Ken Leary, Butch Krattenmaker and Brad Wickes had graduated and Gary Satrappe, who averaged 20.1 points a game as a junior, went to Mainland for his senior year.

Dixie's Raiders were just 3-3 after the first six games of the year. But then they started to roll. Beginning with an 88-33 win over Hammonton and concluding with a 115-51 win over those same Blue Devils, Ocean City won its final 14 regular season games to win its eighth straight CAL title. The team started the NJSIAA Group 2 Tournament by beating Williamstown and Deptford. Next were the defending champions from Salem.

But first, there was "the storm".

"I have very vivid memories of that storm, as you might imagine," said John Cranston, the sophomore point guard. "The funny thing is, I had little awareness it was going to be bad. I went to bed, the storm hit, I woke up, took a shower and dressed for school. I went out on the front porch, which was about three steps up from the street (near 4th and Asbury) and was about to step down when I noticed water sloshing over the porch deck. No school that day.

"Of course, the first thing I thought of was how we were going to practice. Salem was a powerhouse, won the year before and boasted a great player named Jerry Dickerson. Practice time was critical if we were going to have a chance."

Jerry Fadden, the team captain who averaged 17.1 points a game that year, had a similar experience.

"My first recollection was walking out of the house we had on the lagoon at Snug Harbor to go to school that day," he said. "Remember, there was no warning of the storm. Lo and behold, there was the lagoon. Only it was the yard – front and back and all around. So, I had to walk through water to get out and then walked to see how my car was doing (you know, teenagers and their cars). The road was so crowned towards the curb that the water was up to the top of the front wheels. Now, that was scary. It was to get worse.

"Undeterred and thinking a storm is very cool, Jack Hollingshead, Bryan Sherby and I decided to walk down to the Boardwalk at 11th Street in water up to our knees and watch the ocean. This was cool until a wave seemed to come out of nowhere, like a big, huge, open hand, and just grab a whole strip of the boardwalk and all the boardwalk for about 40 feet disappeared along with the store on that corner - 11th and the Boardwalk. It was now literally 11th and the ocean. We decided to beat a tactical retreat, scared out of our wits (assuming we had wits to go there to start with)."

Once the excitement and fear subsided, these guys started to focus on basketball. They hadn't been able to practice for days and the NJSIAA postponed the game a day, hoping they could eventually play.

"Dixie actually got us in the gym for a few minutes," said Cranston, "and they cleared a small space around one of the baskets. It was an evacuation center. We shot a few foul shots but were quickly thrown out. I have this vague memory that a loose ball whacked a kid in the head. We then went down to St. Augustine School to use their tiny gym where we did a walk-through of our offense and some shooting drills, but were unable to practice against opposition. That one practice was it. And Dave Farina could not make any of that because of all the horrible stuff going on in Sea Isle."

"We had no real practice during that period," Fadden said. "We hardly had a gym. Charlie Baker (15.2 points per game), for one, was out rowing around in a boat for several days trying to help people and make it safe. He had a lot of fun trying to shoot a basketball later. Dave Farina (10.7ppg)? We didn't even know if Dave was alive. And my hands were pretty torn up from helping with mooring lines on some of the boats. The tournament people were kind enough to delay our game to at least see if we could show up."

Finally, the Raiders had to head out to play Salem with virtually no preparation.

"When we left for the game," Cranston said, "I recall we had to wait near a field in Upper Township because Dave was being brought by helicopter to meet the bus. It was Dave's stories that finally penetrated my skull and I finally recognized how horrible the whole thing was."

"Wump, wump, wump – all of a sudden a helicopter was landing on this field," said Fadden, "50 feet from our bus. Truthfully very scary. Wump, wump, wump – why a helicopter near the bus? And then we saw - it was Dave Farina. Dixie had somehow arranged to have Dave helicoptered out of Sea Isle to play with his team. Man, were there some wet eyes for that reunion."

That helicopter trip looked different from Farina's point of view.

"I remember being scared to death. I had never flown in anything, much less a U.S. Coast Guard helicopter. My oldest brother, Joe, was a member of the Sea Isle Police Department at the time. He and other policemen got me on the helicopter at what is now JFK Boulevard in Sea Isle City. Upon entering the chopper, one of the coast guardsmen said to me, 'you must know somebody, kid, to get this ride'.

"Once airborne, I became even more frightened than I had been when I saw all of the destruction on the ground and still lots of water everywhere.

"The flight was, I am sure, a very short one, but seemed like an eternity. I really wasn't sure at this point where I was going and who would be meeting me and that, of course, added to my apprehension. Upon landing and exiting the helicopter, I saw three very familiar faces approaching me—Dixie Howell,

Berwyn Hughes and Tom Williams. I think they were almost as happy to see me as I was to see them. Dixie said, 'Dave, are you OK and is your family OK'. I told him we were all fine. He answered, 'Good, now let's hustle. We need to catch a bus'. And catch the bus we did. I will always remember the good feeling of seeing these three people and of seeing guys like Jerry Fadden, John Cranston, Ron Newcomer, Charlie Baker, Dan Money and a certain cheerleader again!

"Ever the coach, Dixie handed me a new pair of white, high top Converse all-star sneakers with my number 20 printed on the back of each sneaker, just like the pair I had been issued at the start of the season. How did he remember my size and how did he think of the fact that I probably lost my sneaks in the storm? Dixie also informed me that I would be guarding the opposing team's best player and it was my job to stop him even if I fouled out of the game. He also told all of the team that it was important to us that we play the game. And we did. The fact is we were soundly beaten and I did foul out of the game. But we played the game.

"I subsequently found out that Dixie, of course, engineered the entire idea of my helicopter ride. It is my understanding that he called in a favor from a friend who was highly placed in the U.S. Coast Guard training center in Cape May to accomplish my evacuation from Sea Isle to play in a tournament game. This event epitomizes what Dixie Howell was all about. I was certainly not the best player on that team. He would have done the same thing for any of his players. It was not about me, it was not about that one game or any one player, it was about the OCHS basketball program and what one man did to make that program one of the best in the state. I was not one of the best players that Dixie ever coached, but he always made me and others who played for him feel that they were. I have always felt that I let him down in that game.

"I believe it is accurate to say that probably never in the history of high school sports anywhere, has a coach gone to the lengths Dixie Howell did to get a very average basketball guard to dry land and have the opportunity to not just play a basketball game, but to have a warm, loving lifetime memory. The events of the 1962 storm certainly affected me and everyone who was a part of it. In many ways, the event itself and the resulting experiences have had a lasting positive impact on my life. My helicopter ride and the real meaning of it remain with me to this day."

"Dave fouled out," Fadden said, "I fouled out, John Cranston could hardly stand up at the end, none of us could do much of anything even closely resembling basketball."

The Raiders lost to Salem, 64-46.

"I'd like to say we would have won if we had had a chance to practice as usual," Cranston said, "but I strongly doubt it. Pretty sure it would have been a better game, though. Salem was a great team and went on to win the group championship for the second year in a row."

The 1961-62 school year was one of change. But the basketball and swim teams at OCHS were champions and the groundwork was being laid for more success in the future.

Chapter Four

1962-63

A lot of interesting things happened in 1962-63.

The school year started with three moments that would impact the entertainment business for a long time. On Sept. 11, the Beatles recorded their first single, "Love Me Do". On Oct. 1, Johnny Carson took over as host of "The Tonight Show". And, a few days later, the very first James Bond film – "Dr. No" – made its debut.

In January, George Wallace became Governor of Alabama and promised "segregation now, segregation tomorrow and segregation forever." In March, Attorney General Robert Kennedy ordered the Alcatraz Penitentiary in San Francisco Bay closed. In April, General Hospital debuted on ABC-TV and Rev. Martin Luther King Jr. was arrested in Birmingham, Alabama for parading without a permit. In June, Pope Paul VI succeeded Pope John XXIII and President John Kennedy gave his famous "ich bin ein Berliner" speech in West Germany.

"Lawrence of Arabia" won the 1963 Oscar as best picture. Tony Bennett's "I Left My Heart In San Francisco" was the record of the year. The best supporting actor on TV was Don Knotts as Barney Fife on "The Andy Griffith Show". The Yankees beat the Giants in a seven-game World Series. In pro football, the Packers beat the Giants again for the NFL championship. Loyola-Chicago defeated Cincinnati to win the NCAA basketball title and ended the Bearcats two-year hold on the title. The Celtics topped the Lakers a second straight year to win the NBA championship. And Julius Boros won a three-way playoff with Arnold Palmer and Jack Cupit to win the U.S. Open golf tournament.

In Ocean City, Andy Prohaska's football team got off to a great start. The Raiders defeated Holy Spirit, 7-0, in the season opener when Jim Wimberg took a short pass from John Burch and turned it into a fourth quarter touchdown. After a tie with Woodstown in a non-league game, Ocean City registered a 39-0 win over Wildwood, the defending Cape-Atlantic League champion. Nick Alise ran for 117 yards and two touchdowns with Burch, Jack Bello and Earl Tarves also scoring.

The following week it was a 21-7 win over Lower Cape May with Harry Brown and Dan Money running for TDs and Burch connecting with Bob Mayer for the other. Then OCHS defeated Hammonton, 33-7, with Money rushing for 166 yards and two scores. Bello, and Tarves also ran for TDs with Burch connecting with Alise for another. After five weeks, Prohaska's Raiders were 4-0-1 and had outscored their opponents, 106-20. But Oakcrest, and South Jersey's leading scorer, George Spivey, was waiting.

Spivey scored three touchdowns and threw for the other as the Falcons handed Ocean City its first defeat, 27-13. Burch and Brown scored for the Raiders, who then sandwiched a win over Middle Township between losses to Mainland and Pleasantville. The victory over the Panthers allowed Ocean City to claim the mythical Cape May County championship.

When the awards were announced at the end of the season, Dave Rollins was selected to the CAL's first team all stars. Bello finished his career with 791 career rushing yards, one of the five highest totals recorded by an OCHS back.

The basketball season began with a pair of victories for Dixie Howell's team. The Raiders defeated Millville and Mainland in December. John Burch led the way against Millville with 16 points and Charlie Baker's 16 led three double-figure scorers against the Mustangs. Ocean City also defeated Pleasantville, 52-42, with Burch scoring 15.

Just before the Christmas break, the team dropped a 67-64 decision to its alumni in a game that didn't count. In those days, colleges would allow their players to play in games like that during holiday breaks. Ken Leary, back from Boston University, stole the show with 10 points and 14 assists. Brad Wickes (Hartford) scored 22, Jerry Fadden (Penn) had 16 and Mike

Fadden (Bucknell grad) scored 11. Bill Haynes led the Raiders with 12 points, John Cranston scored 11 and Ed McClain 10.

After beating Manasquan in a non-league game over the holidays, Ocean City lost its first game, 53-50, to Holy Spirit, which was led by Tom Walker's 22 points. Baker had 14 points and 16 rebounds for OCHS. Dixie's team then won three straight – over Hammonton, Wildwood and Oakcrest – before losing to Mainland, 46-43, in the rematch.

The Raiders wrapped up the Cape May County title with consecutive wins over Lower Cape May, Middle Township and Wildwood. Baker poured in 31 points against the Tigers and scored 27 against Wildwood. OCHS also defeated Oakcrest before the four-game win streak was ended by Pleasantville, 68-66. The Raiders beat Lower and Middle again and topped Shore Regional in a non-league game with Baker grabbing 29 rebounds. They lost a 64-63 non-league decision to Millville, which was coached by Jack Boyd, who would succeed Dixie as the OCHS coach a few years later.

When the Raiders defeated Hammonton they finished in a tie with Pleasantville for the CAL title. A playoff game was scheduled at Mainland and the Greyhounds ended the OCHS eight-year streak of championships with a 46-44 win in overtime. Free throws by John Hunt and John Essl in the final 34 seconds of the extra period were the difference.

After losing the CAL playoff in such a tight game, Dixie was concerned about his team's final regular season game. The Raiders were going to Pennsauken to face Bishop Eustace Prep, coached by future NBA coach Don Casey and one of the highest ranked teams in South Jersey. If Ocean City was beaten badly in this game his fear was that the team would not be in the right frame of mind to start the NJSIAA Group 2 Tournament.

So, Dixie decided to have his team freeze the ball.

It was 0-0 after one quarter and the Raiders led, 5-3, at the half. Eustace managed to outscore Ocean City, 10-7, in the third quarter to take a 13-12 lead. A free throw by Burch was the only point in the fourth quarter and it was 13-13 after regulation time. The first overtime was scoreless but Pete Johnston, who years later would return to coach Eustace, scored in the final seconds of the second overtime to win the game, 15-13.

The Raiders started the Group 2 Tournament with a 63-48 win over Delsea at Vineland with Cranston scoring 19 and Baker 18. That advanced them to the second round against undefeated Salem and Dixie decided to use the freeze tactics again. But Salem, having obviously heard about the game with Eustace, was prepared. The Rams led, 13-9, at the half, forcing Ocean City to attack the basket. Eventually, Salem notched its 23rd straight win, 44-38, to end the OCHS season. Salem's all-star center, Jerry Dickerson, scored 17. Burch got 11 for Ocean City.

Baker averaged 15.9 points and 15.7 rebounds per game, becoming the sixth Ocean City player in school history to average a double-double. Burch and Cranston averaged over nine points each with Burch leading the team in steals and Cranston in assists. Money averaged 11.3 rebounds per game.

While the basketball team was creating excitement on the hardcourt, the swim team put together another record-breaking season. Fenton Carey's team finished 12-2 and finished its dual meet season by defeating Moorestown, ending the Quakers' 65-meet win streak.

The Raiders finished third in the prestigious Princeton Relays and were fourth in Group 2 at the NJSIAA State Meet. Fenton Carey Jr. (above) had a record-breaking year, not only writing his name into the OCHS record books but also setting a state record in the 100 yard breaststroke. He became the first Ocean City swimmer to win a state championship. The medley relay team of Bob Thompson, Carey, Art Carr and Fred Klein also set a new state group record in their event.

Ocean City swept Atlantic City, the only other area school with a swim team, and therefore won the Bruce Presti Memorial Trophy again. Over parts of three seasons, Carey's swim team had compiled a record of 28-3.

Charley Mumford got the baseball season started on the right foot when he shut out Mainland, 6-0, on two hits in the opener. Mumford struck out 15 and retired 14 straight at one point. He also had two hits and drove home two runs. The Raiders followed that up by beating George School, 11-4, with Ed McClain delivering three hits and driving home five runs.

The Raiders added wins over Hammonton and Wildwood before losing to Atlantic City, 7-0, when Bill Haynes' single was their only hit. Head coach Dixie Howell missed the games when he was hospitalized with a bleeding ulcer. Assistant coach Fred Haack took over in his absence. Ocean City bounced back from the loss to the Vikings to beat Wildwood, 4-1. Mumford and John Wilson combined to limit the Warriors to one hit and Mumford smacked two home runs. They then topped Lower Cape May, 5-0, on a no-hitter by Wilson, also beat St. Augustine Prep, 9-1, and were 8-0 winners over Middle Township in a game that featured a grand slam by Haynes.

Pleasantville edged the Raiders, 2-1, in an important game late in the season that was a pitcher's battle. Mumford limited Pleasantville to two hits, a single and a triple by Bob Williams, who scored one run and drove home the other. Winning pitcher John Essl allowed five OCHS hits, including two each by Mumford and Frank Chattin.

Ocean City was eliminated in the first round of the NJSIAA Group 2 Tournament by Edgewood, 6-1, despite the four-hit pitching of Wilson. Four of Edgewood's runs were unearned. Mumford had a single and a triple for OCHS. The Raiders followed with a 3-0 win over Middle Township on Mumford's two-hit, 17-strikeout performance. Dave Mazzoni clubbed a long home run as Ocean City clinched a tie for the CAL championship.

In the final game of the baseball season, Mumford tossed a no-hitter, striking out 12, as OCHS defeated Mainland, 2-0. Ocean

City managed only three hits off the Mustangs' Joe Sundra, singles by McClain, Haynes and Gene DeHaven.

Mumford completed one of the great seasons in school history. He was 7-3 with a 0.96 earned run average, striking out 108 in 65 innings. In his three losses, the Raiders scored just one total run and committed 11 errors. At the plate, Mumford led the team with a .462 average, 17 runs batted in, eight extra base hits and eight stolen bases. McClain hit .358 and Chattin .320.

Fenton Carey's track team opened with a 63-36 win over Mainland. Dan Money led the way with wins in the 100, 200 and broad jump. Ray Healy added firsts in the shot put and discus. After splitting two meets, the Raiders defeated Lower Cape May, 77-22. Ocean City finished first in eight events – Jim Groogan in the 100, Jim Gleeson in the 220, Earl Tarves in the 440, Mark Baum in the mile, Charlie Baker in the high jump, Money in the broad jump, Healy in the discus and Tom Wimberg in the javelin.

This would be Coach Carey's final season as Ocean City High School track coach. In 11 seasons, his teams were 52-13 in dual meets, winning eight Cape-Atlantic League championships and two South Jersey titles.

The 1962-63 school year saw excitement on the football field, on the basketball court and in the pool. And it finished with a championship baseball team and the end of an era in track.

Chapter Five

1963-64

Some memorable things happened during the 1963-64 school year.

In November, the President of the United States – John Fitzgerald Kennedy – was shot and killed during a motorcade in Dallas. Vice-President Lyndon Johnson was given the oath on Air Force One and became the 36th President. All television and most radio suspended normal programming and either played uninterrupted music or provided coverage of the aftermath of the assassination, the procession of World leaders with the horse-drawn casket to the Capitol Rotunda and the funeral. Two days later, the accused assassin was murdered on live television. Ocean City schools were closed following the president's death for a day of mourning.

In January, Sen. Barry Goldwater announced he would seek the Republican nomination for President. In February, the Beatles appeared on "The Ed Sullivan Show", putting Beatlemania into overdrive. In March, "Jeopardy" debuted on NBC-TV. In May, cable television came to Ocean City. In June, George Meyer retired as Ocean City High School principal and was replaced by Mike Subotich. And on Father's Day, the Phillies' Jim Bunning pitched a perfect game.

"Tom Jones" won the 1964 Oscar as best picture and Sidney Poitier became the first black actor to win the Academy Award. The record of the year was "Days of Wine & Roses" by Henry Mancini. The Emmys for comedy actors on TV went to both Dick Van Dyke and Mary Tyler Moore from "The Dick Van Dyke Show". The Dodgers, led by Sandy Koufax, swept the Yankees in the World Series. In pro football, the Bears beat the Giants for the NFL championship and the Chargers topped the Patriots to win the AFL title. John Wooden got his first NCAA Basketball Title when UCLA defeated Duke. The Celtics made it six straight NBA titles, beating the Warriors in five games. And Arnold Palmer won the Masters for the fourth time in seven years.

Andy Prohaska's football team had only an eight-game schedule. They started it – and finished it – with tie games.

The opener was a 14-14 tie with Holy Spirit when the Raiders rallied from a two-touchdown deficit. Earl Tarves scored a second quarter TD and Jim Wimberg ran 65 yards for the tying score in the third period. Jim Gleeson gained 94 yards rushing in the game.

The season-ending tie was 12-12 with Pleasantville on Thanksgiving morning, just six days after President Kennedy was killed. Tom Herrington and Wimberg are pictured, above, with Coach Prohaska prior to the Thanksgiving game. Note the flag behind them was still at half-mast because of the President's death. Gleeson ran for 124 yards and one TD with Wimberg scooping up a fumble and running for the other TD. Pleasantville tied the game in the fourth quarter when quarterback John Essl connected with Pete Elco.

In between, the Raiders were 3-3. They lost to Wildwood, 26-13, with Meredith Campbell leading the Warriors. They defeated Lower Cape May, 33-13, with Gleeson running for 249 yards and Tarves for 124 as OCHS set a school record with 539 yards total offense. Then, it was a 46-25 win over Hammonton with Tarves gaining 109 yards and six different players scoring.

Oakcrest beat the Raiders, 20-7, with George Spivey scoring twice. Tarves gave Ocean City the early lead with a 33 yard TD run. The third OCHS win was the first ever over Mainland after losing the first two seasons. Quarterback Joe Kish (6-for-8, 92 yards) threw two TDs, one to Tom Herrington and one to Bud Swan, and Ed McClain's two extra points were the difference in a 14-12 win. The Raiders then lost to Middle Township, 14-7, after taking the early lead on Gleeson's first quarter TD run.

Fenton Carey's swim team started the winter season with a win over Haddon Heights, led by Fred Klein's double victory. Klein touched first in the 100 yard freestyle and 100 yard backstroke. The Raiders got wins from five different swimmers in defeating Asbury Park and won every event, including two each by Klein, Art Carr and Bill Lafferty, in a comfortable victory over Wilmington (DE) High School.

The OCHS swimmers won the Bruce Presti Memorial Trophy again by beating Atlantic City. They also finished fourth in the South Jersey Invitational in Margate. The 200-meter freestyle relay team of Klein, Ken Guiles, Ken Penska and Bill Johnson finished first.

Ocean City followed with an impressive 48-47 win over the highly-ranked Valley Forge Military Academy. A first and second by Ken Ryan and Bob Young, respectively, in the 100 yard breaststroke clinched the win for Carey's team. Lafferty was a double winner in the impressive victory.

The Raiders finished 10-3 and Klein set school records in the 40 yard freestyle, 50 yard free, 100 yard backstroke, 45 yard freestyle and 105 yard backstroke. The unusual distances were in home meets where OCHS competed in the 15 yard pool tucked between the locker room and the gymnasium. It was believed to be the smallest pool used by any high school in the country for competition.

The biggest news in the winter season came in March when Dixie Howell's basketball team won the NJSIAA State Group 2 championship, only the second state team title in school history. The Raiders defeated North Arlington, 76-51, in the Atlantic City Convention Hall to complete a five-game march through the group.

Randy Fox sparked the state championship victory with a remarkable 21-point performance. John Cranston added 19 points, Ed McClain got 15, Barry Banks scored 14 and Bill Haynes added seven as the five players who had largely carried this team through the season were all key contributors in the final game.

Cape May County schools were a big force in the state final weekend on the Atlantic City Boardwalk. In addition to Ocean City's win in Group 2, Wildwood won the Group 1 championship, 83-65, over Wallington. And Wildwood Catholic dropped a 68-63 decision to Holy Family in two overtimes in Parochial Class C. Ironically, neither of the two state champions – Ocean City nor Wildwood – won the Cape-Atlantic League. Mainland won the CAL title in a special tie-breaking playoff game over Wildwood.

Ocean City reached the state final by beating Dunellen, 74-49, in the state semifinal at Asbury Park Convention Hall on St. Patrick's Day. Cranston led four players in double figures with 22 points.

The Raiders won the South Jersey championship, the fourth in school history, by beating Glassboro, 71-62. Cranston scored 20 points with both Haynes and McClain grabbing 26 rebounds.

The state tournament began with a 62-50 win over Sterling in which Haynes had 13 points and 35 rebounds, a new OCHS single-game rebound record. McClain added 12 points and 22 rebounds.

Next up was a 76-55 win over Bordentown with all five Ocean City starters scoring in double figures. Haynes added 21 rebounds, McClain grabbed 19 boards and Cranston had 10 assists, giving the Raiders three double-doubles in the game. That win moved OCHS into the South Jersey final.

Mainland, the CAL champion, had beaten the Raiders twice during the regular season. The Mustangs won, 51-46, with Bud Wertley getting 19 and Skip Castaldi 17, in December. And Mainland won, 57-55, in the second meeting in January with Bud and Dick Wertley combining for 37 points.

The Raiders split with state champion Wildwood – losing, 61-55, despite Cranston's 27 points, the first time around and then edging the Warriors, 61-59, in the rematch when Fox made two free throws with six seconds left.

In January, Ocean City defeated Middle Township, 71-45, for Dixie Howell's 200th career victory. Cranston scored 23 with Fox and Banks each getting 14. Six-foot-six Ted Croitor had 29 points for the Panthers.

Ocean City played three challenging non-league games in the final 10 days of the regular season. The Raiders defeated St. Joseph of Camden, 88-83; beat Haddonfield, 70-55; and lost to Atlantic City, 70-60. McClain scored 28 points in the win over St. Joe. Cranston scored 26 in the loss to Atlantic City, which ended the OCHS win streak at 10 straight. Cranston had 20 points and Haynes had 14 points and 17 rebounds against Haddonfield.

Cranston completed one of the greatest seasons in OCHS history with the state championship. He finished with 451 points, the second highest single season total in school history. His 119 assists was a school record for a season and he finished four shy of Ken Leary's career assist record. Cranston scored 800 points in his career. He was selected second team, all-state and McClain joined him on the first team, All-Group 2. Haynes became the seventh player in school history to average a double-double.

The spring season started with Dixie's baseball team beating Hammonton, 9-2, on a three-hitter by Ron Beaver. Ken Guiles had a double and two singles and Bill Haynes blasted a home run. Beaver got another win in relief when his sacrifice fly scored Rick Howell, who had doubled and advanced on a ground out, with a walk-off run in a 7-6 win over George School. Beaver got his third mound victory, 3-2, over Hammonton and Ed McClain made his first high school start as a pitcher a successful one in an 8-5 win over Middle Township.

The Raiders then faced two of the best pitchers in South Jersey – Cal Butler of Pleasantville and Will Beauchemin of Holy Spirit – and split the two decisions. McClain shut out the Greyhounds on seven hits for a 1-0 win. The only run scored when Butch Milligan brought home Beaver on a suicide squeeze. But Beauchemin was too much, striking out 13 and allowing just four hits in an 8-0 win by the Spartans.

McClain pitched a two-hitter as Ocean City defeated Lower Cape May, 2-0, and the Raiders lost the rematch with

Pleasantville, 10-9, despite hitting four home runs. Beaver homered twice with McClain and Jim Wimberg also hitting for the distance. Rick Howell beat Wildwood, 11-1, in his first pitching start and then the Raiders rallied two days later to beat the Warriors again, 14-9. Haynes had three hits and drove home four runs.

McClain beat Mainland, 7-3, with a three-hitter as Guiles had three hits for OCHS. And then, in the final week of the season, the Raiders won two games that clinched the CAL title for the eighth time in 10 seasons. They defeated Middle Township, 5-1, on a three-hitter by McClain, who had three hits himself. And they defeated Lower Cape May, 7-6, in 13 innings. Beaver scored the winning run on an error and McClain threw seven shutout innings in relief.

McClain, Beaver and Milligan were all named first team, All-CAL. McClain hit .333 and was 7-1 on the mound with a 1.95 earned run average. Wimberg hit .326, Milligan .324, Guiles .313 and Joe Kish .292. Beaver was 4-1 as a pitcher and led the team in RBIs, extra base hits and runs scored.

New track coach Ted Klepac started his career with a 71-19 victory over Oakcrest with Earl Tarves, Ken Thompson and Bud Swan each winning twice. The Raiders followed that by upsetting Middle Township, 51-45, despite getting only four first places – by Thompson, Randy Fox, Mark Baum and Jim Gleeson. Ocean City also defeated Mainland, 58-41, with six different Raiders winning events.

The Raiders defeated Wildwood, 59-40, despite three wins by the Warriors' Meredith Campbell. Swan (shot put), Gleeson (javelin) and Frank Mazzitelli (discus) swept the throwing events. Campbell later led Wildwood to the CAL championship by also winning three events. Baum won the mile, the only OCHS athlete to win at the CAL meet, which came the day after the Ocean City Prom.

It was a school year that began with an international tragedy but included championships by Dixie Howell in both basketball and baseball, including his 200th career basketball win; a fantastic basketball season by John Cranston; the debut of Ted Klepac as track coach; and the great versatility of Ed McClain, an all-state basketball player, successful kicker in football and one of the best baseball players in South Jersey.

Chapter Six

1964-65

There were high points and low points during the 1964-65 school year.

In July, Don Pileggi was named to succeed the retiring George Gardiner as Ocean City's Recreation Director. Gardiner, a descendant of The Lake Family that founded the resort, earned national recognition for his recreation programs during his 22 years as director. Then, a little over a month later, Gardiner died suddenly at the age of 60. He was a 1923 graduate of Ocean City High School who also graduated from the Wharton School at the University of Pennsylvania. While at Penn, Gardiner was an NCAA gymnastics champion.

In September, the Phillies had a 6 ½ game lead in the National League with 12 games left before losing 10 straight and finishing second. In October, the Summer Olympics opened in Tokyo. In November, President Lyndon Johnson was elected to a full four-year term, getting more than 60 percent of the vote against Sen. Barry Goldwater. In December, Dr. Martin Luther King was awarded the Nobel Peace Prize. In January, Sir Winston Churchill died of a stroke in England at age 90.

And, in March, the Ocean City Convention Hall on the Boardwalk at Sixth Street was completely destroyed by fire. It was not only a building that housed many events, especially throughout the summer, but it was were basketball players of all ages and all sizes gained experience and honed their skills in the VFW Youth Leagues and weekend pickup games.

"My Fair Lady" won the 1965 Oscar as best picture and Julie Andrews, who played the lead in the musical on Broadway but was passed over for the film lead, won the Academy Award as best actress for another film – "Mary Poppins". The record of the year was "The Girl from Ipanema" by Astrud Gilberto and Stan Getz. The Emmy for best comedy series on TV went to "The Dick Van Dyke Show" for the third straight year. The Cardinals, who won the National League pennant after the Phillies' collapse, beat the Yankees in a seven-game World Series. In pro football, the Browns beat the Colts for the NFL championship and the Bills defeated the Chargers to win the AFL title. UCLA won its second straight NCAA Basketball Title, beating Michigan in the final. But the real excitement at the Final Four came from Princeton forward Bill Bradley who, despite playing for a third place team, was named the Final Four MVP. He scored 58 points in winning the consolation game over Wichita State. The Celtics made it seven straight NBA titles, beating the Lakers in five games. And Jack Nicklaus won the Masters.

After losing the football opener to Holy Spirit, 7-0, in a game that featured the famous Joe Kish jump pass attempt, the Raiders got the offense going in a 31-12 win over Merchantville. Earl Tarves scored twice with Craig French, Kish and Ron Fox each crossing the goal line once. That was followed by 27-13 loss to Wildwood when Meredith Campbell ran for 96 yards and one touchdown while throwing two others to Jim Waicus. Kish scored both of the Raiders TDs.

With Kish missing with an injured back, Ocean City dropped to 1-3 when Lower Cape May beat them, 13-7. A 50-yard TD run by French in the fourth period was the only score. The Raiders followed with a pair of wins over Hammonton and Oakcrest. Three runners went over 100 yards rushing against Hammonton – French (107), Tarves (100) and Ken Thompson (100) – with Tarves and Thompson each scoring twice.

In the win over Oakcrest, Griff Reese blocked a Falcon punt at the end of the game's first series. Ron Beaver recovered the ball on the Oakcrest 10. Tarves gained eight yards on two carries, including the 1,000th yard of his career, Thompson added another and French got into the end zone on fourth down. Tarves threw a conversion pass to French to give the Raiders all the points they would need – or get. The two-point conversion had not yet become a rule in 1964.

The following week the fumble went against the Raiders. Prohaska switched his team into a single-wing type formation because of the season-ending injury to Kish. It worked well, with Tarves (above) gaining 110 yards as the tailback. But an Ocean City fumble was recovered in the end zone by Mainland's Larry Royal in the fourth quarter and the Mustangs came away with a 7-0 victory. George Landis protected that lead with an interception in the final minute, his second of the game.

Next was a 27-6 loss to Middle Township, a win that allowed the Panthers to clinch the Cape-Atlantic League championship. Bud Swan caught a 44 yard TD pass from Tarves in the second quarter to tie the game at halftime. But Middle had a 21-0 advantage in the second half to wrap up its title.

The Raiders went into the Thanksgiving game with Pleasantville not only missing Kish but Tarves and Beaver, as well, because of injuries. And Jim Gleeson was just back after missing four games. The Greyhounds prevailed, 31-7, with French rushing for 67 yards and the only OCHS score.

Tarves would finish his career with 1,140 rushing yards, the second highest recorded total in OCHS history. The highest was the 1,259 by his brother, Don. Swan was named to the CAL first team all stars.

The loss to Pleasantville would be the final game for Prohaska as OCHS football coach. His teams were 13-19-3. After stepping down as coach of the Raiders, he would take over as head coach at Mainland in the fall of 1965.

The winter season began with a win by Fenton Carey's swim team as Bill Lafferty and Chris Labs won twice in a 69-26 win over Haddon Heights. In one of Lafferty's wins he set a new school record in 105 yard butterfly, breaking the old mark set by Norm Ervine. Lafferty won twice again in a win over Camden County Tech. Lafferty doubled again in a win over Girard College.

Ocean City beat Atlantic City to clinch the Bruce Presti Memorial Award as Lafferty won twice, including breaking his own butterfly record. Ken Penska set a new school mark in the 60 yard freestyle. Dennis Carey doubled for OCHS in a win over Haddon Township and Lafferty finished first twice in a win over Pennsauken.

The Raiders edged always tough Asbury Park, 52-43, with Chris Danser and Ken Ryan taking first places and Marlin Howe winning the diving. The victory might have been more comfortable but Lafferty was disqualified in the butterfly, his strongest event. He began to experience the loss of his swim trunks and, when he stopped to adjust them, he broke form.

Carey's team finished 11-4 and, in addition to the individual school marks by Lafferty (butterfly), Penska (60 free) and Ryan (105 breaststroke) set a school record in the 180 freestyle relay. The record-setters were Danser, Penska, Dennis Jones and Bill Johnson. That same relay team supplied Ocean City's only first place in the NJSIAA Class B Meet, helping the team to an overall third place finish.

Dixie Howell's basketball began defense of its state championship with a 67-42 win over Millville with John Laudenslager scoring 24 points. But, after nine games, the Raiders were 5-4, having lost twice to Mainland and once to Wildwood. In the first loss to the Mustangs, Skip Castaldi scored 29 points for the Mustangs and Randy Fox got 19 for OCHS. The Raiders placed five in double figures in a win over Hammonton and beat Pleasantville behind Barry Banks' 21 points.

In a holiday tournament for the dedication of Atlantic City's new gymnasium, the Raiders rallied to defeat Memorial of West New York, 56-50. Fox fouled out with three minutes left in the first half but Laudenslager scored 17, Craig French 13 and John Moore 12. The win moved the Raiders into the tourney final where they lost to Atlantic City, 72-63. In a 75-62 loss to Wildwood, Laudenslager scored 21 but the Warriors' Chuck James had 26. Wildwood went on to win the CAL championship.

Ocean City started a three-game win streak with a win over Oakcrest, despite 22 by the Falcons' 6-6 center, Ernie Wynn. That was followed by a 63-61 overtime win over Pleasantville when Fox hit a jumper with nine seconds left in overtime to tie the game, then stole the ball and was fouled as time ran out. He made the two free throws to win the game. The Raiders followed that with a 62-50 win over Lower Cape May as Moore and Rick Howell each scored 15.

The Raiders got ready for the NJSIAA Group 1 Tournament with a pair of wins at the end of the regular season. They defeated Valley Forge Military Academy with Laudenslager's 18 pacing four in double figures. And Howell scored 21 in beating Holy Spirit with four in double figures again.

This NJSIAA tournament would be challenging since Ocean City had been dropped back into Group 1 by the association, meaning they would have to contend with another state champion – Wildwood, which had already beaten the Raiders twice. The season before, OCHS had won the state Group 2 title and Wildwood had won in Group 1.

But there were other games to win before worrying about the Warriors. Ocean City opened the tournament with a 70-51 win over Glassboro. Laudenslager scored 20, Banks 17, Moore 13 and Howell 10. The Raiders then defeated Bordentown, 65-57, with Banks scoring 28 and Fox 13.

Those two wins moved OCHS into the South Jersey final at Glassboro State College where they would, indeed, meet Wildwood. The Warriors had won the first two games by a combined 25 points. This one would be different.

Ocean City rallied from a 10-point deficit in the first half and tied the score on Howell's layup with nine seconds left in the fourth quarter, sending the game into overtime. But the Wildwood combo of Chuck James, Jim Waicus, Meredith Campbell and Harry Hayward was too much and the Warriors came away with a 63-58 win and the championship.

Ocean City finished 15-9. Laudenslager (14.3), Banks (13.0) and Fox (12.4) all averaged in double figures. Moore averaged 9.8 points and 10.2 rebounds a game. French made 79 percent of his free throws, Banks made 99 steals and Fox had 101 assists. Fox finished his career with 701 points and Banks scored 564.

In one of the most exciting contests of the spring season, the Raiders edged Lower Cape May, 5-2, in eight innings when Butch Gleason delivered a two-run single in the eighth. It was Gleason's second hit of the game. John Kiphorn also had two hits. Ron Beaver went the distance and was the winning pitcher.

Mainland beat the Raiders in eight innings, 3-1, on a two-hitter by the Mustangs' Jay Law. Beaver and Kiphorn had the lone hits. Rick Howell smacked a two-run home run in a three run fifth inning to beat Wildwood, 5-3. Beaver got the win and Herb Bond the save. Larry Masi had two hits. Beaver also got the win over Middle Township, 4-1, despite only getting three hits – by

Bond, Howell and Gleason. The Panthers' lone run came on Chuck Dougherty's home run.

Following three CAL championships in four years, the OCHS baseball team finished just 5-9 in what would be the final season for head coach Dixie Howell. In 13 seasons, his teams were 117-56.

Ted Klepac's track team finished fourth in the CAL Championship Meet. Mark Baum was the only Raider athlete to win, taking first in the mile run. John Laudenslager scored points in three events – fourth in the high jump, fourth in the broad jump and fifth in the 220 yard run. Others to score for OCHS were Bud Swan, second in the shot put; Herm Scheibein, third in the high jump; Les Bratton, fourth in the mile; Walt Hughes, fourth in the discus; Ron Fox, fifth in the broad jump; and Jim Talmadge, fifth in the pole vault.

But the Raiders demonstrated their depth, winning the CAL Relays a week later on their home field. Ocean City won the shot put relay with the quartet of Swan, Hughes, Craig French and Charley Wirtz. The Raiders were also first in the broad jump relay with Fox, Laudenslager, Wirtz and Ken Thompson.

Chapter
Seven

1965-66

Change was in the air in 1965-66.

In its five sports, for example, Ocean City High School had two new head coaches. John Cervino, the freshmen football coach at the University of Pennsylvania, replaced Andy Prohaska as head coach of the Raiders. Prohaska had moved across Great Egg Harbor Bay to Mainland. And Fred Haack, a longtime OCHS baseball assistant, took over that program when Dixie Howell retired to become the school's full-time athletics director.

The Ocean City High School campus was changing, too. The school year was filled with the sounds of drills and hallways that led to nowhere as the 40-year old building was expanded in all directions.

Elsewhere, Sandy Koufax pitched a perfect game for the Dodgers in September, his fourth no-hitter in four seasons. And Fidel Castro took over in Cuba. In April, a uniform daylight savings time is enacted. In May, Walt Disney World in Florida debuted the "It's A Small World" ride and a new Ocean City hotel – the Port-O-Call – opened on the Boardwalk at 15th Street. In June, "The Dick Van Dyke Show" ended its five-year run on CBS. And, also in June, the National Organization for Women was founded.

"The Sound of Music" won the 1966 Oscar as best picture. The record of the year was "A Taste of Honey" by Herb Alpert. The Emmy for best actor in a TV series went to Bill Cosby for "I Spy". The Dodgers beat the Twins in a seven-game World Series. In pro football, the Packers beat the Browns for the NFL championship and the Bills and defeated the Chargers to win the AFL title. In the NCAA Final Four at College Park MD, the championship game was one that changed things and became the subject of books and films. Texas Western, an all-black team, defeated all-white Kentucky and its racially motivated coach, Adolph Rupp. The game changed attitudes toward black players and opened up recruiting, especially in the south. The Celtics made it eight straight NBA titles, beating the Lakers in seven games. And Jack Nicklaus won the Masters for the third time in four years.

Before the football season started, the Archie Harris Booster Club was formed by parents Bob French and Jack Neall, pictured below with Coach Cervino. The group, named for the former great OCHS athlete, met regularly at the Plymouth Inn to support the team and honor players.

Cervino's football team, loaded with sophomores, dropped its first three games, including a 27-7 loss to Wildwood. The lone OCHS score was a TD pass from Bob Glaspey to Jim Holt. The Raiders notched their first win when John Henry scored twice – from 89 yards and 80 yards – in a 12-6 win over Lower Cape May. But that was just the beginning for Henry.

The following week he scored five times, all in the first half, in a 50-20 win over Hammonton. Henry scored from 62 yards away then, in quick succession, from nine, 55, 62 and 64 yards. He also caught a pass from Glaspey that went for 53 yards to the Hammonton 19. After being shut out by Oakcrest, the Raiders faced Mainland – and their former coach, Andy Prohaska. The former coach and his Mustangs got the best of them, 39-12. George Landis scored three times for Mainland and Jim Swanseen hit Bert Horton twice for scores. Glaspey ran for one OCHS touchdown and hit Ken Penska for the other. The Mustangs went on to finish undefeated and win the CAL title.

The Raiders were shut out by Middle Township the next week and went into the Thanksgiving game with Pleasantville needing a win to finish the season on a positive note. And they got it! Henry scored Ocean City's only TD in a 7-6 win and Glaspey hit Holt for the extra point that was the difference. Tony Washington recovered two Pleasantville fumbles to help keep the Greyhounds' offense under control.

The winter sports season started with a tragedy. OCHS senior Laura Montagna was killed in an automobile accident just days before the first contests. The basketball team started with a 59-57 loss to Mainland and the swimmers were beaten, 51-44, by Philadelphia's Cardinal O'Hara in their opener. Both teams were filled with athletes still in mourning. John Moore scored 17 and Rick Howell 14 for the basketball team. Ken Penska and Chris Danser were winners in the swim opener.

The basketball team would not lose again for more than two months.

That included a 79-43 win over Mainland less than a month later. The Raiders took a 21-7 lead after one quarter and 43-17 at halftime. Howell scored 28, Ron Fox 20 and Moore 18. In subsequent games, Moore scored 21 more when Ocean City defeated Oakcrest; Howell poured in 24 in a win over Middle Township; and Fox scored 21 in a non-league victory over Eastern.

Moore scored 18, Howell 16 and John Stuempfig scored 12 in a 76-59 win over Wildwood, giving them a sweep of the Warriors. They stretched their win streak to 10 games with an 89-51 win over Lower Cape May with Moore getting 19 points, Fox and Howell 16 each.

The Raiders clinched the CAL championship with a 75-24 win over Hammonton. Moore scored 19, Fox 18, Howell 14 and Stuempfig 10. It was the 11th league championship for Ocean City and the ninth under Dixie Howell.

OCHS stretched its winning streak to 15 games with a 59-39 win over Haddonfield. Moore scored 19 and Howell added 18. They wrapped up the regular season by beating Oakcrest, 70-39, with Stuempfig scoring 24 points and Howell adding 14.

Pitman was up first for the Raiders in the NJSIAA Group 1 Tournament and Ocean City was a 71-52 winner. Howell scored 25 points, Fox added 15, Moore 12 and Stuempfig 10. Next was Kingsway and the Raiders buried them, 65-36, for their 18th straight win. It was the third longest winning streak in OCHS history. All four OCHS starters scored in double figures – Moore scored 15, Stuempfig had 13, Howell scored 12 and Fox and Tony Washington each got 10.

But Ocean City faced Williamstown in the South Jersey Final at Camden Convention Hall and the streak would end, 45-41, despite 17 points by Howell and 12 by Fox. It was the third straight year that the Raiders would reach the South Jersey final.

The Raiders finished 18-2 with Howell averaging 18.6 points, Moore 15.0 and Fox 14.8. All three of them were named first team, All-CAL. Howell finished his career with 654 points.

The swimming team also put together some impressive victories. They defeated Camden County Tech, 77-16, when Penska set a new school record in the 60 yard freestyle. Chris Pfaeffli was a double winner as the Raiders defeated Girard College, 75-20. Penska bettered his own freestyle record in a 60-35 win over Asbury Park. Mike Myrhe remained undefeated in the diving competition and OCHS also got wins from Pfaeffli, Danser, Ken Gorman and Mark Bacon.

The Raiders out-swam P.S. duPont High School of Wilmington, 75-20. Danser and Dennis Carey were double winners in the victory. They beat Valley Forge Military Academu, 61-34, with Carey doubling again. The 400 yard freestyle team – Danser, Penska, Bill Johnson and Pfaeffli – set a new school record. And Carey added another double win in a 79-16 win over Pennsauken. Penska, Gorman and Jim Hogan were winners in a

56-39 loss to Cherry Hill. And the Raiders dropped a decision to Moorestown.

Carey's team would finish second in the NJSIAA Championship Meet at Princeton University with Danser, Penska, Johnson and Pfaeffli (above) winning a state championship in the 400 freestyle relay.

Ocean City started Fred Haack's first season as head baseball coach with a 1-0 win over Middle Township. Butch Gleason singled in the fifth, moved to second on a walk and the speedy outfielder raced home on a throwing error. Rick Howell earned the shutout win, limiting Middle to four hits. The Raiders made it 2-0 with a 5-1 win over Lower Cape May. Howell got the win in relief. Gleason and Larry Masi each had two singles.

Masi provided Haack's team with its next win, a 3-2 victory over Wildwood in eight innings. He opened the eighth with a single, stole second and was bunted to third by Dave Beyel. When Frank Kruk hit a ground ball back to the mound, Masi broke for home. He collided with the catcher, who dropped the ball, and OCHS had won.

Ocean City notched another win, beating Hammonton, 2-1, on Howell's three-hitter. Singles by Beyel and Bill Jones drove home the two OCHS runs. But the Raiders lost to Holy Spirit, 4-2, on a four-hitter by the Spartans' Rich Halverson. A 6-0 loss to Pleasantville followed when the Greyhounds' Dennis Hood pitched a one-hitter. That one hit was a single by Beyel.

The Raiders rallied in the seventh for another walk-off win when they defeated Lower Cape May, 7-6. Trailing by one run entering the bottom of the seventh, Beyel lashed a triple and scored the tying run on Gleason's single. A walk to Ken Ferrier moved Gleason to second and he raced home with the winning run on Chris Pfaeffli's single. Beyel had four hits in the game and Dave Faragher got the win in relief.

Middle's George Schwartz limited the Raiders to four hits in a 2-0 shutout win. Two of the hits were by Jones. And Pleasantville's Hood stopped them again, pitching a two-hitter in a 14-1 win by the Greyhounds. The Raiders finished the season with a 6-2 loss to Mainland. George Landis reached base all four times, including a home run, for Mainland. Howell homered and Pfaeffli had two hits for OCHS.

On the track, Ted Klepac's team defeated Mainland, 64-44, to start the season. Ron Fox was a double winner, in the 440 yard run and broad jump, with Gary Harmon winning both the 100 and 220. The Raiders also surprised Middle Township, 55-52, with Fox and Harmon again doubling. And doubles by Fox and Harmon also led to an 80-28 win over Pleasantville. Charles Wirtz (shot put), Pat LaRosa (discus) and Bill Goetz (javelin) swept the throwing events.

John Henry was the focus of the Raiders' 84-23 win over Wildwood. He ran the 100 yard dash in 9.9 seconds, breaking a school record that had stood for 16 years. Henry also won the 220. Fox also doubled again for Ocean City.

Klepac's team successfully defended its CAL Relay title, beating second place Wildwood, 49-28. Ocean City won three events in the meet. Henry, Harmon, Bob Elia and Jim Tarves combined to win the half-mile relay in meet record time. Fox, Wirtz, Ken Penska and Ward Abronski won the mile relay and the quartet of Fox, Harmon, Penska and Jeff Curtin won the broad jump relay.

In the season's final dual meet, OCHS defeated Lower Cape May, 63-42. Henry and Fox doubled with Goetz (javelin) and Frank Williams (two mile run) also finishing first.

Chapter Eight

1966-67

Consistent performances by John Henry and Ken Penska and a high-scoring basketball game were a few of the highlights of 1966-67.

Elsewhere, in September, "Star Trek" made its debut on NBC-TV and probably has run on some station – either with original episodes or reruns – every day since. In December, Walt Disney died while producing "The Jungle Book", the last feature to be created under his personal supervision. In January, the United States Post Office Department made zip codes mandatory. In February, the 25th Amendment to the U.S. Constitution, covering presidential succession, was ratified. And, in May, Elvis Presley married Priscilla Beaulieu, whom he met in Germany while serving in the military.

Also in May, Bob Sharp, Dave Simpson and Robinson Chance were elected as the Ocean City Commissioners for four-year terms. Sharp was chosen to be the new mayor.

"A Man for All Seasons" won the 1967 Oscar as best picture. The record of the year was "Strangers in the Night" by Frank Sinatra. The Emmy for best comedy series went to "The Monkees". The Orioles swept the Dodgers in the World Series. In pro football, the Packers beat the Cowboys for the NFL championship and the Chiefs topped the Bills in the AFL title game. But there was something new – the two champions of the pro football leagues played each other for the first time in the AFL-NFL Championship Game. Two years later the name would be changed to Super Bowl. Vince Lombardi's Packers won this first game, 35-10, over the Chiefs.

UCLA, led by sophomore Lew Alcindor, was back in the NCAA Final Four and the Bruins defeated Dayton in the championship game. It was Coach John Wooden's third national title in four years. In the NBA, the Philadelphia 76ers ended Boston's streak of eight straight NBA titles, beating the Celtics in five games to win the Eastern Conference. The Sixers – led by Wilt Chamberlain, Billy Cunningham and Hal Greer – then defeated the Warriors in six games and Philadelphia had its first NBA champion in 11 years.

At OCHS, John Henry started the football season by scoring three touchdowns in the opener, the final one on a 60 yard run. But the Raiders did not convert the extra point after that final score and had to settle for a 19-19 tie with Eastern. Ocean City played another non-league game the following week and dropped a 12-7 decision to St. James of Carney's Point. Henry scored the only OCHS touchdown in that one.

The first win came in the season's first Cape-Atlantic League game, a 38-7 win over Wildwood and it was quarterback Bob Glaspey who led the way. Glaspey threw four touchdowns – one each to Henry, Ken Penska, Frank Kruk and Jim Holt – to wrap up the victory. Larry Masi and Ellis Ford ran for the other Ocean City scores.

Next was Lower Cape May and John Cervino's team escaped with a 7-6 victory. Trailing, 6-0, Jim Tarves ran 23 yards for a TD in the third quarter and Jim Toresdahl kicked the crucial extra point. The Raiders had moved over .500 with a 2-1-1 record but were undefeated in the league. Hammonton was next.

The Blue Devils handed Ocean City its first league loss, 14-7. It was Hammonton's first win over the Raiders in a decade. Glaspey connected with Penska on a 54-yard scoring play that produced the lone OCHS touchdown. After a 6-0 loss to highly-rated Washington Township came a 29-7 loss to Mainland with George Landis scoring three times for Andy Prohaska's Mustangs. Henry scored the Raiders' TD.

A 20-14 win over Middle Township ended the three-game losing streak. Glaspey threw TD passes to Penska and Holt and Henry ran 60 yards for the third, and decisive, score. The Raiders had a chance to finish with a .500 record on Thanksgiving but were beaten, 31-14, by the Greyhounds. Archie Robinson scored three times for Pleasantville. John Henry scored the two Ocean City touchdowns, including a 91-yarder that set a new school record for the longest TD run. He scored his second following a fumble recovery by Ted Kensil.

The basketball team had the same problems at the start of its season, losing its first two games to Millville and Mainland. The Raiders got their first win, 55-35, over Pleasantville with Dave Beyel scoring 14 points and John Moore 13, and then defeated Hammonton, 76-31. Following a snow storm that gave Ocean City its first White Christmas since 1912, the Raiders lost to North Jersey power Clifford Scott from East Orange and defeated Germantown (PA) Friends in a pair of home games over the holiday break.

The Raiders started the new year with a four-game win streak that included a non-league game with Oakcrest, plus CAL wins over Mainland, Lower Cape May and Middle Township. Beyel scored 26 points and Moore 21 in an 83-56 win over Lower and Franz Adler's double-double (15 points, 16 rebounds) led the way over Middle. After a second loss to Wildwood, the Raiders started a six-game win streak by beating Oakcrest, 49-43, with Moore getting 17 and Beyel 12.

That streak of victories included a 45-35 win over Pleasantville, with Moore scoring 18 and John Huff 12; a 47-40 victory over Middle Township, sparked by Moore's 24 points; and a 58-38 win over Valley Forge Military Academy, with Moore getting a double-double with 18 points and 13 rebounds. After a loss to Millville stopped the win streak, the Raiders began to focus on the NJSIAA Tournament. They had moved back up to Group 2 and they were scheduled to open with always-tough Salem. But first, they had a regular season game left against Hammonton.

And what a game it was! Ocean City defeated the Blue Devils, 119-43, setting a new school record for points scored in one game. It marked the seventh time OCHS had scored 100 or more points and broke the record of 115 set against Hammonton five years earlier. The Raiders scored 64 points in the first half, including 40 points in the second quarter. Moore led the scoring with 25 points, Huff scored 18, Howell got 17, Adler 16 and Beyel and Stu Shriner each scored 15.

Ocean City followed that outburst with a 51-32 win over Salem in the first round of the tournament. Moore scored 15 with Beyel and Huff each adding 13. But Gloucester City knocked the Raiders out of the tournament with a low-scoring 38-29 decision. Moore led Ocean City scoring with 11 points.

Moore and Beyel, pictured below, had memorable seasons. Moore finished with a double-double for the season, a 15.6 scoring average and a 10.8 rebounding average. Beyel scored 12.3 per game. Beyel made an impressive 73 percent of his free throws. Moore graduated with 860 career points which, at the time, was the second highest total in school history behind Ken Leary.

The swim team had another great season, finishing 13-2. One of those wins was over Brandywine (DE) High School in which Ken Penska, Chris Danser and Dennis Carey each doubled. In addition, Jim Hogan set a new school record in the 105 yard backstroke. They beat Atlantic City to win the Bruce Presti Memorial Award again. Penska and Carey were both double winners in the meet. And they defeated Valley Forge Military Academy with Penska and Carey each doubling up again. One of Carey's win was a school record in the 300 yard freestyle.

Ocean City lost a close meet to the powerful Peddie School, 51-44, despite two first place finishes by Danser and a one-two finish in diving by George Busfield and Tag Hughes. But they bounced back to win the New Jersey Coast Championship Meet, in competition with 11 other teams at Monmouth College. Penska won the 50 freestyle and the quartet of Hogan, Alan Richter, Ken Gorman and Chris Pfaeffli won the 400 freestyle.

The Raiders finished second in the NJSIAA State Meet at Princeton with Penska setting another record in the 50 freestyle. They finished off their season by defeating a team that had always given them trouble with a 54-41 win over Moorestown. Both relay teams were winners against the Quakers and the Hughes-Busfield combo was one-two in diving. Penska, Gorman and Hogan were individual race winners.

Ted Klepac's track team opened its season with a 69-58 loss to Woodbury, Klepac's alma mater and the school where his father was a highly successful coach. Ken Penska won the long jump, Buddy Abrams won the high jump, Bill Milligan was first in the pole vault and Charles Wirtz was declared the winner of the 440 yard run when the Woodbury winner was disqualified.

Ocean City won its second dual meet, blasting Mainland, 72-36. John Henry swept the two sprints and Penska finished first in the 440 and broad jump. The Raiders also defeated Middle Township, 79-28, with Henry and Penska again winning twice. Henry tied his own school record with a 9.9 seconds time in the

100. And Henry doubled again in a 64-44 win over Pleasantville. Penska won the long jump, John Woodrow added a win in the 880, Les Bratton the two-mile and Jack Neall the shot put.

In the Cape-Atlantic League Relays, Klepac's team won four events to win the championship. Henry, Gary Harmon, Bob Scheibenz and Ken Southard combined to win the half-mile relay. Penska, Wirtz, Doug Jones and Richard Booth won the mile relay. Bratton, Woodrow, John Shaw and Lou Taccarino won the two-mile relay.

Ocean City also won the CAL Championship Meet with three Raiders taking first place. Henry won twice, taking the 100 and 220. He set a meet record in the 220. Bratton won the two-mile, also setting a meet record. And Penska had the best long jump.

The Raiders' lost their final dual meet of the season, 80-45, to Oakcrest. Henry doubled in the sprints, putting up another 9.9 in the 100. Ocean City bounced back to defeat Holy Spirit, 91-17, by winning every event. Penska won the 440 and long jump with Abrams taking the high jump and discus. Then they finished off the regular season 6-2 after a tri-meet win over Lower Cape May and Hammonton. Henry and Penska were double winners.

The OCHS baseball team, under Fred Haack, started the season by scoring four runs in the top of the seventh to defeat Wildwood, 9-5. Dave Faragher got the win in relief. John Huff, Frank Kruk, Dave Beyel and Larry Masi each had two hits. The Raiders followed with a 5-2 loss to Middle Township when the Panthers' John Muller pitched a three-hitter. Harry Richards had two of the OCHS hits. Ocean City later defeated Wildwood again, 7-0, on a one-hitter by Faragher, who struck out 10. Kruk had a double and two singles, Bob Taylor singled twice, Beyel smacked a home run and Masi and Bud Rinck both doubled.

In a 6-5 win over Middle Township, Faragher came on in relief in the top of the seventh with the Panthers leading, 5-2. He struck out the side. Then, in bottom of the seventh, Faragher hit a walk-off home run to complete a four-run OCHS rally.

Chapter Nine

1967-68

At Ocean City High School, the 1967-68 school year brought a football championship back to its hallways and included a high-scoring basketball team that reached another South Jersey final in the final season of a legendary coach.

But there was a lot more in this school year, including some tragedy.

In October, however, Delaware Valley sports fans had a new pro team to follow. The Philadelphia Flyers debuted in the National Hockey League. The Flyers lost their opener, 5-1, in Chicago with a starting lineup by Coach Keith Allen that included Brit Selby on the left wing, Wayne Hicks on right wing, Lou Angotti at center, Jean Gauthier and John Miszuk as defensemen and Bernie Parent in goal. The team finished that first season 31-32-11 and was led in goals by Leon Rochefort.

In March, Senator Robert Kennedy announced his candidacy for President of the United States and, a couple weeks later, President Lyndon Johnson declared that he "shall not seek, and will not accept, the nomination of my party for another term as your President." In April, Rev. Martin Luther King was murdered in Memphis TN. And, in June, Robert Kennedy, moments after being declared winner of the California Democratic Primary, was shot in the head in the kitchen of Los Angeles' Ambassador Hotel. He died the next day.

"In the Heat of the Night", which later became a very good TV series starring Carroll O'Connor, won the 1968 Oscar as best picture. The record of the year was "Up, Up and Away" by Marilyn McCoo and the 5th Dimension. "Get Smart" and lead actor Don Adams both were Emmy winners in comedy. The Cardinals beat the Red Sox, 4-3, in the World Series, despite the presence of triple crown winner Carl Yastrzemski. In pro football, the Packers beat the Cowboys for the NFL championship and the Raiders topped the Oilers in the AFL title game. In the AFL-NFL Championship Game, the Packers won easily again, 33-14, over the Raiders.

In the NCAA Final Four, UCLA made it two straight and four in five years by defeating North Carolina in the championship game. In the NBA, the Boston Celtics won their ninth NBA title in 10 years, beating the Lakers in six games. The Montreal Canadiens swept the St. Louis Blues to win their third NHL Stanley Cup in four years.

The Cape-Atlantic League football season started off in rather impressive fashion. Ocean City defeated St. Joseph of Toms River, 58-6, scoring more points in one game than any OCHS team since 1944, when the Raiders defeated Wildwood, 63-0. Jim Tarves scored twice; Bob Glaspey scored once and threw a TD to Jim Foglio; Tom Bond connected with Frank Kruk on a 91 yard TD that set a record for the longest TD pass play in school history; Dan McElyea ran for a score; and the final points went on the board when Bruce Beaver scooped up a St. Joe fumble on the OCHS 39 yard line. His eyes widened at the open field before him and he ran 61 yards for a touchdown. It almost seemed like the play was in slow motion and some observers were concerned that darkness might set in before Beaver would cross the goal line. But his points wrapped up an Ocean City romp.

John Cervino's team followed with another non-league victory, a 27-19 win over St. James of Carney's Point. Glaspey threw three touchdowns in the game, two to Tarves and one to Foglio. Jack Neall added the final score when he returned an interception 37 yards.

The Cape-Atlantic League opener was a little tougher as the Raiders edged Wildwood, 13-7. And they had to come from behind to do it. Halfway through the fourth period, Ocean City trailed, 7-0. But Glaspey hit Tarves for 45 yards to move deep into Wildwood territory. Glaspey then scored on a four yard run. The extra point try was unsuccessful, however, and the Warriors still led, 7-6. But Dave Beyel later intercepted a pass and made a strong return to the Wildwood four yard line. Glaspey went over from there and also ran for the extra point.

Next was a 33-0 shutout of Lower Cape May that lifted the Raiders to 4-0. Larry Masi scored a pair of touchdowns, Glaspey scored one and hit Tarves for another and Hank Adams ran for a TD. The Raiders went on to defeat Hammonton, 45-13, with Masi scoring twice and Neall returning an onside kickoff for a TD. McKean (DE) High School came to town next and left after a 24-7 win by Ocean City. Glaspey scored once and threw a TD to Foglio, Masi ran for a touchdown and Adams ran 91 yards with the opening kickoff of the second half.

Ocean City's six-game win streak came to an end in Linwood when Mainland won a 13-12 decision. Masi and Glaspey scored for the Raiders, Ed Masters and Steve Parker scored for MRHS. Denny DiOrio kicked the extra point that was the difference. After the loss, the Raiders needed wins in their two final games to win the CAL championship.

They defeated Middle Township, 13-6, on a tie-breaking touchdown by Glaspey in the second half. He had completed a 59 yard TD pass to Tarves in the first half. This result, complete with Pleasantville's win over Lower Cape May, left the two teams – OCHS and Pleasantville – tied for first and made the Thanksgiving Day game a championship game for the first time. Ocean City won it, 13-7, with Glaspey scoring both TDs and the Raiders won the league title for the first time in 10 years.

Or, at least, that was what everybody thought as they ate Thanksgiving dinner that night. But, about five weeks later, it was discovered that Hammonton had used an ineligible player during its tie game with Mainland. The Mustangs were awarded with a victory in that game, tying them with the Raiders for the CAL championship.

Neall, above with Principal Mike Subotich, was named to the All-State Team by the Newark Star-Ledger.

Ocean City did not open the basketball season until after Jan. 1. Coach Dixie Howell was told by Subotich that this was the way the schedule would be arranged in the CAL in the future but he was wrong. The schedule went back to normal the following year but without Howell. He would retire after the 1968 season to become the school's first full-time athletics director.

The extra rest before starting might have helped, though, as the Raiders kicked off the season with a 101-62 win over Lower Cape May. Terry Howell scored 18 points, Stu Shriner 17, John Huff 14 and Dave Beyel and Larry Masi 10 each. Ocean City then defeated Deptford, 71-40, with Howell scoring 19 points; and Mainland, 57-45, with Howell and Huff combining for 27 points. Then they had another high-scoring effort, beating Hammonton, 106-44, with Beyel scoring 20 points and Adler 19, leading five in double figures.

The Raiders' five-game undefeated streak was snapped by Pleasantville, 60-55, despite 19 by Beyel. The Greyhounds rallied back from a five-point deficit in the fourth quarter. Middle Township followed with another win over Ocean City, 53-51, behind 27 points by Stedman Graham, who would, years later, became a highly successful educator and author who earned international recognition as the longtime companion of Oprah Winfrey.

Dixie's team got back on the winning track with wins over Wildwood and Lower Cape May. Howell and Buddy Abrams each had 14 against Wildwood and Nick Trofa tossed in 28 points against Lower. The Raiders later bounced back to beat both Pleasantville and Middle in the rematches. Beyel scored 30 against Pleasantville and Glenn Darby led the scoring against Middle with 18 points.

The Raiders finished the regular season with two wins. They beat Oakcrest, 66-62, and were 114-54 winners over Valley Forge Military Academy. Beyel led the scoring with 20 against Oakcrest and 26 against Valley Forge. The Raiders had six in double figures against Valley Forge and became the first team in OCHS history to score 100 or more points three times in the same season.

Ocean City finished in a three-way tie for the CAL championship with Wildwood and Mainland so a playoff was arranged. Mainland won the toss and received a bye. The Raiders played Wildwood at Pleasantville and dropped a 65-61 decision despite Beyel's 22 points. Mainland then defeated the Warriors, 78-74, in the CAL title game.

In the NJSIAA Group 2 Tournament, Ocean City defeated Palmyra, 76-51, with Beyel scoring 22, and then edged Gloucester, 58-53, behind another 22 by Beyel. That moved OCHS into the South Jersey final for the fourth time in five seasons. The Raiders faced Penns Grove in the championship game and fell behind by 13 points in the first quarter en route to a 65-54 loss. Huff paced OCHS with 13 points in what was the 346th and final game coached by Dixie Howell. He would retire with a record of 277-69, the most wins by a CAL coach.

Sandwiched around losses to Holy Spirit and Asbury Park, the OCHS swim team, now coached by Jim Hutchinson, defeated Atlantic City, 51-44. John Taccarino, Bill Struckell, Don Hamilton and Tom Barrett won swimming events with George Busfield winning the diving competition. In the loss to Asbury Park, Hamilton won twice, Tom Kruegl was a winner in the 100 breaststroke and Busfield won the diving. In a 63-32 loss to Lenape, Busfield was the top diver for the fifth straight meet.

Busfield added another win and Ocean City bounced back with a 69-25 win over Merchantville with Lou Barrett winning twice and Struckell winning the 100 butterfly. The Raiders also beat Wilmington's P.S. duPont, 61-34, with Struckell doubling and Busfield remaining undefeated. A 58-37 win over Cherry Hill East featured wins by Busfield, Hamilton, Struckell, Barrett and Dan Montagna. But they lost to Cherry Hill West (Cherry Hill had split into two high schools) despite wins by Kruegl and John Pfaeffli. Busfield did not win the diving, ending his winning streak at eight meets.

Moving outdoors in the spring, the OCHS track team lost to Middle Township, 70-55, despite double wins by Buddy Abrams (120 hurdles and high jump) and Jack Neall (shot put and discus). They bounced back to beat Hammonton, 91-35, with Hank Adams putting together a triple – winning the 100, 200 and long jump. Neall again won the shot and discus. They lost to Pleasantville despite wins by Adams, Abrams, Neall, Bill Martin, Gary Blizzard and Dan Curtin.

Ocean City lost to Mainland, 93-33, with the Raiders' Doug Jones sharing the 100 yard win with Adams and also winning the long jump. Neall won the shot put. Mainland went on to win the CAL Championship Meet, beating Middle Township by 10 points. OCHS was sixth with Neall winning the CAL shot put.

The OCHS baseball team started its season with a trio of losses. Hammonton beat them, 11-1, with Dave Beyel getting two singles. They lost to Middle Township, 1-0, on a four-hitter by George Schwartz. Dave Faragher also pitched a four-hitter, striking out 10, in a losing effort. Tom Bowen and Tim O'Shea each had two hits for the Raiders. And they lost to Hammonton again, 8-5, in a game shortened to five innings by rain. Bowen had three hits.

Ocean City notched its first win, 5-4, over Lower Cape May in nine innings. The walk-off run scored when Beyel singled, stole second, moved to third on Masi's fly ball and scored on Bowen's sacrifice fly. Beyel, Kruk and Brian Broadley each had two hits. Bowen, who drove home the winning run, pitched all nine innings and struck out 16. Masi blasted a long home run in a 5-0 win over Middle Township as Bowen struck out 12 and pitched a five-hit shutout.

The Raiders defeated Wildwood, 6-2, when they were limited to a pair of singles by Warriors' pitcher Steve Korzeniowski. Beyel and Masi got the two hits and OCHS scored five unearned runs to make Faragher a winning pitcher. Ocean City finished the season by blasting Lower Cape May, 15-0. Beyel had a home run and two singles, Bowen and Broadley each had three singles with Masi, winning pitcher Bowen and Bud Rinck each delivering two hits.

At the end of the school year, in June 1968, the Youth Center was closed. This building, across Atlantic Avenue from the high school, had been the city's tennis club during the summer but was generally empty during the school year. Then, in 1953, Don Pileggi returned from military service and convinced the city to allow him to create a real youth center in that tennis building. George Loder joined him a few years later and, for 13 years, that building became the social home of teenagers from Ocean City and other communities.

Chapter Ten

1968-69

Things changed in Ocean City during 1968-69. There was a new basketball coach, a full-time athletics director and a new spring sports team. There were lots of changes elsewhere, too.

In September, a new television news show – "60 Minutes" – debuted on CBS. In November, Republican Richard Nixon was elected the 37th President of the United States, defeating Democrat Hubert Humphrey by a little more than 500,000 votes. In January, the Beatles gave their last public performance together on the roof of Apple Records in London.

The year 1969 is frequently referred to as "the year everything changed." There were anti-war demonstrations, some becoming violent, all across the country. Apollo 11, carrying Neil Armstrong, Buzz Aldrin and Michael Collins, landed on the moon. Followers of Charles Manson brutally attacked and killed seven people in Los Angeles, including actress Sharon Tate. And The Woodstock Festival was held on a farm in upstate New York.

"Oliver!" won the 1969 Oscar as best picture. The record of the year was "Mrs. Robinson" by Simon & Garfunkel. "Get Smart" and lead actor Don Adams both were again Emmy winners in comedy. The Tigers surprised the Cardinals, 4-3, in the World Series, led by 31-game winner Denny McLain and Mickey Lolich, who won three games in the series. In pro football, the Colts beat the Browns for the NFL championship and the Jets defeated the Raiders in the AFL title game. In the AFL-NFL Championship Game, after quarterback Joe Namath guaranteed victory for his Jets against all odds, the Jets did defeat the Colts, 16-7, with Wildwood High School graduate Randy Beverly playing a key role as a defensive back.

In the NCAA Final Four, UCLA continued to roll, winning its third straight title and fifth in six years by defeating Purdue in the championship game. The Boston Celtics also continued their domination, beating the Lakers, 4-3, for their 10th NBA title in

11 years. The Montreal Canadiens again swept the St. Louis Blues to win their fourth NHL Stanley Cup in five years.

The OCHS football season started with a 21-0 win over St. Joseph of Toms River. Skip Given returned a punt 47 yards for one score and then ran 18 yards for another. Hank Adams added the third TD when he returned an interception from 18 yards out. Next was a 25-13 win over St. James with Tom Bond scoring two fourth period touchdowns after throwing a pair of TDs to Adams. One of those touchdown pass plays covered 91 yards, tying the school record Bond had set the year before.

The Raiders opened play in the Cape-Atlantic League by beating Wildwood, 44-14. Given returned another punt for a score and added two more TDs on runs from scrimmage. Buddy Abrams ran for one TD and caught another from Bond. And Dan Town scored the final TD. That win was followed by a 6-0 victory over Lower Cape May in a constant rainfall. Abrams caught a six-yard TD pass from Bond in the first period for the game's only score.

Ocean City's four-game unbeaten streak ended when Hammonton shut them out, 27-0. But, after a week off, the Raiders fashioned their own shutout at Recreation Center Field against Mainland. On the first offensive play of the game, Bond connected with Abrams for a 67-yard touchdown. Neither team would score again and OCHS limited the Mustangs to 41 yards of total offense and won, 6-0. It was the only time the Raiders would beat their former head coach, Andy Prohaska.

The following week, Bond threw three touchdowns in a 33-12 win over Middle Township. Bond hit Adams twice and Abrams once for scores. Abrams and Tom Kravitz each also ran for touchdowns. On Thanksgiving morning at Ty Helfrich Field in Pleasantville, the Raiders were beaten by the Greyhounds, 20-6. Bond hit Abrams for the only score in the fourth quarter after an interception by John Huff.

Bond, Abrams and center Gary Gans were selected to the All-CAL offensive team. Adams and Brian Broadley were named to the defensive all star team. Huff, with his great instincts and in his first varsity football season, set a school record with 11 recoveries in a season. He also tied a school record for interceptions in one game and tied another for recovered fumbles in a game.

Both winter teams had different head coaches from the previous season.

Jack Boyd, the freshmen coach in 1968 and a former head coach at Millville, was named by Dixie Howell, the new OCHS athletics director, to succeed him as basketball coach. A basketball assistant from the previous year, Pete Horn, also left and later became head coach at Washington Township.

And Fenton Carey returned as coach of the OCHS swim team after a one-year absence when Jim Hutchinson left to accept a job at his alma mater, Southern Regional High School. Hutchinson was a very successful athlete at Southern and was inducted into the school's Hall of Fame in 1992.

The swimmers started with a tight 48-47 loss to Pennington Prep, despite wins by Don Hamilton (50 yard freestyle), Bill Struckell 100 butterfly), Steve Brown (100 backstroke), John Pfaeffli (200 individual medley) and George Busfield (diving). Ocean City got a win over Camden County Tech and then finished second in the Haddon Township Relays.

A 68-27 win over Atlantic City gave OCHS the upper hand in the battle for the Bruce Presti Memorial Award. Dave Bruce was a double winner for Carey, taking the 105 breaststroke and the 180 individual medley. The Raiders lost to Cherry Hill West, 67-38, despite a pair of wins by Hamilton. A win over Asbury Park also featured a double by Hamilton. And Struckell doubled in a 67-28 win over Holy Spirit.

The Raiders defeated P.S. duPont from Delaware, 71-22, with Hamilton, Struckell and Lou Barrett each notching two wins. Busfield continued his success with another diving victory. Ocean City then surprised Moorestown, 55-40, with Barrett winning twice and clinched the Presti Award by beating Atlantic City again with Hamilton winning two events. The Raiders won, 61-34, against Cherry Hill East with Hamilton getting his seventh double of the season and Barrett his third. Busfield, a defending state champion, was out with a neck injury that would end his season. And they upset Valley Forge Military Academy, 52-43.

Ocean City won the New Jersey Seaboard Invitational at Monmouth College, beating out 12 other teams. The Raiders finished first in the two relays. Pfaeffli, Steve Brown, Tom Kruegl and Tom Bond won the 200 yard medley relay. Bond, Jim Dull, Tom Clark and Buzz Hickman won the 400 freestyle relay.

The basketball team gave Boyd wins in his first six games, starting with a 57-56 conquest of Oakcrest. The Raiders beat Croydon Hall, 90-69, with six players in double figures; they defeated Lower Cape May, 87-65; edged Mainland, 69-65; topped Hammonton, 87-47, with Gene Davis getting 18 points and Glenn Darby 18; and beat Sacred Heart, 60-54, Darby and John Huff each scoring 16.

Pleasantville – coached by former Atlantic City High School and Harlem Globetrotter star, Gene Hudgins – ended the OCHS win streak with a 53-40 win. The Raiders bounced back with an 80-78 overtime win over Middle Township when Tom Bowen made a pair of free throws with two seconds left. Middle's Stedman Graham scored 40 points, including a bucket at the end of the fourth quarter that sent the game into overtime. Huff and Darby each had 18 for Ocean City.

The Raiders lost to Wildwood, 65-64, when Mike James completed a three-point play in the final seconds. Bowen had 19 for Ocean City. Mike Korzeniowski had 21 and Ernie Troiano 13 for Wildwood. A 56-52 loss to Paul VI followed with Huff scoring 12. After wins over Hammonton and Lower Cape May, Boyd's team took on Wildwood Catholic, which, like Sacred Heart, was in its first season as part of the Cape-Atlantic League.

Ocean City defeated Wildwood Catholic, 63-47, behind Bowen's 22 points. The game was interrupted with three minutes left in the first half when police cleared the OCHS gym because of a bomb scare. The Raiders also defeated Wildwood, 85-70, in the rematch with Huff (above) scoring 20 points. Huff got 17 in a 53-46 win over Sacred Heart and tossed in 24 in a 66-57 win over Middle Township. But Pleasantville was next and the Greyhounds beat the Raiders again, 74-53.

OCHS wrapped up the regular season by defeating Oakcrest, 60-53, with Terry Howell scoring 20, and then losing to Washington Township, 66-62. The Raiders were one of four teams involved in a special CAL playoff that was necessary because Wildwood Catholic and Sacred Heart joined the CAL too late to schedule every team twice. Ocean City drew Wildwood Catholic in the first round and dropped a 43-34 decision to the Crusaders, who went on to win the title in their first season in the league.

The Raiders defeated Clearview, 71-54, in the opener of the NJSIAA Group 2 Tournament and then topped Bordentown, 72-50. They met Washington Township, coached by Sal Paone, again in the third round at Glassboro State College and dropped a 66-64 overtime decision. Darby scored 20 points in a losing effort. There were a couple of problems with the scoreboard clock in the game that the officials had to correct.

Ocean City finished 16-7. Huff was a first team CAL all star and led the team with a 14.9 scoring average. He was also the team leader with 80 steals and 75 assists. Darby averaged 12.9 points and 10.7 rebounds on the season and Bowen averaged 11.9 points.

Bowen started the baseball season the way he ended the basketball season. He pitched a four-hitter in beating Wildwood Catholic, 12-5. Tim O'Shea and Brian Broadley each had three hits. The Raiders lost to Oakcrest, 8-0, on Tim Flamingo's one-hitter. The lone hit was a fourth inning single by Bruce Beaver. Ocean City lost to Middle Township, 2-1, despite two hits by Bowen.

Fred Haack's team followed with a pair of 1-0 victories. Bowen shut out Hammonton on one hit, though he walked seven and had to pitch out of bases loaded situations twice. The OCHS run scored when Beaver singled home Terry Howell. The Raiders then defeated Pleasantville behind Bowen's two-hit shutout, getting the only run when Gary Yentsch brought home Huff with a suicide squeeze. Another great pitching performance followed when Yentsch and Bowen combined to no-hit Wildwood in a 5-2 win. Yentsch loaded the bases with one out in the seventh inning and Bowen came on to strike out the final two hitters.

Ocean City lost to Pleasantville, 6-1, in the rematch despite a double and single by Huff. Mainland beat the Raiders, 9-2, despite two hits each by Howell and James Gayle. Bowen did a little bit of everything in an 8-0 win over Sacred Heart. He pitched a three-hit shutout, struck out 11 and drove home four runs, including a two-run homer. Beaver also hit a home run for the Raiders. OCHS lost to Lower Cape May, 4-2, despite two hits each by Howell, O'Shea and Gayle. The Raiders were blanked by Lower Cape May, 1-0, when Bowen retired the first

16 batters but gave up a walk-off home run in the seventh. Beaver paced OCHS with two hits.

The OCHS track team opened the season by beating Mainland, 79-48. Gene Davis was a triple winner, in the 400 hurdles, long jump and high jump. Hank Adams swept the two sprints. After a loss to Oakcrest, Ocean City defeated Pleasantville and Wildwood. John Fitzick won the 100 and 200 in both meets. The Raiders followed that up by winning the Cape-Atlantic League Relays and finishing second to Pleasantville in the CAL Championship Meet. Fitzick won the 220 and Dan McElyea was first in the discus.

Ocean City won both ends of a tri-meet, beating Hammonton and Lower Cape May. Davis was a double winner. He also won twice in a loss to Holy Cross and in a 72-54 win over Middle Township. One of the highlights of the season was the record-setting efforts of Jim Wilson, who set school and CAL records for the two-mile run.

This was the first year of tennis at OCHS and the team finished 4-8 under Coaches Rod Bosbyshell and Dixie Howell. Scott Hand, Bob Cramer and Bill Creighton were the three singles players.

More sports were to come in the next decade including varsity teams for girls.

Chapter Eleven

Before 1960

The CAL during the 1960s – particularly Ocean City High School's involvement within it – has been covered in the first 10 chapters of this book. But there was a great deal of success at OCHS in the years before the 1960s.

For example, OCHS football teams won the first three CAL championships, the first two (1949-50) under Coach Fenton Carey and the third (1951) under Ed Cardner. Carey also coached the Raiders to back-to-back CAL football titles in 1956-57. In addition, during the NJSIAA's pre-playoff days, Ocean City teams were awarded South Jersey football championships in 1932, under Coach Von Henroid; in 1945, under Coach Wilbur Clark; and in 1948, under Carey.

The Ocean City-Pleasantville football series was always important. And there were some exciting highlights. In 1923, quarterback Tony Selvagn scored the only OCHS touchdown in a 6-6 tie. Art Camp and Joe Broadley both scored in a 14-7 win in 1925. Charles Adelizzi scored seven points in a 13-0 win in 1927, the year Babe Ruth hit 60 home runs. Ocean City beat the Greyhounds, 31-0, in 1929 with John LePore scoring three times. In 1931, Walt Kensil scored twice and OCHS won, 21-0. In 1932, Romeo Adelizzi scored twice in a 24-0 win that ended an undefeated season. Bob Wallace scored twice in the Raiders' 12-0 win in 1933. In 1936, Joe Elbertson ran 20 yards for a fourth quarter TD and a 7-0 win.

Jumping ahead to 1948, the Raiders won, 6-0, when Joe Avis hit Walt Buckholtz for the only score. Buckholtz scored three times the following year for a 32-7 Ocean City win. In 1956, Al DeSantis ran 95 yards with a kickoff in a 20-7 victory. In 1957, Ed Adamczyk and Don Balsley scored in a 13-7 win. Bill Shallcross accounted for both TDs in the 13-0 win in 1958, running for one and passing to Chet Loveland for the other.

There were some great individual accomplishments. George Loder intercepted three passes and had four total recoveries in one game. Al Whiteside recovered three fumbles in one 1958 game, six in a season and nine in his career, all school records. Don Mulford returned an interception 100 yards for a 1944 touchdown. Joe Broadley ran 95 yards with a fumble for another touchdown.

Andy Jernee put up impressive rushing and passing numbers in the late 1950s. His teammate, Walt Buckholtz, was equally remarkable. Charles and Romeo Adelizzi scored a combined 441 points in the mid-1930s. Le Pore scored what was a school and South Jersey record 84 points in 1929. Adamczyk led South Jersey scoring in 1957.

In basketball, Ocean City won the CAL championship in 1950-51 in a season of two coaches. Carey coached the first two games before leaving for military service. Cardner completed the season. Dixie Howell became coach in 1952-53 and, two years later, his teams began a string of eight straight CAL titles.

The Raiders, led by Jim Isard, Walt Buckholtz and Bert Avis, were South Jersey Group 2 champions in 1951. The trio of Joe Kennedy, Frank Wickes and Chick McDowell led them to the school's first state team championship in 1955. And, in 1957, the Raiders, led by Tom Adams, Wayne Hudson and Mike Fadden, were 23-0 and South Jersey titlists before losing in the state final.

Another undefeated regular season followed in 1957-58, led by Fadden and Larry Harrison, which ended with a 71-69 loss in the South Jersey final. Wayne Thompson and Phil Huber sparked the 1955-56 team to a CAL title. Ed Keenan averaged 18.4 points per game in 1948-49, a school record at the time, and joined with Joe Myers for a 17-2 season and the very first CAL championship.

In 1942, under Coach John Carey, the Raiders, led by Charles Bringhurst and Bill White, were 14-2 and reached the South Jersey final. In 1938, Nick Guarracino and John Huff helped the Raiders, coached by Von Henroid, to the South Jersey final. They were also South Jersey finalists in 1937, led by Dick Fox.

Charles Adelizzi and Lou Carey were both named All-South Jersey in basketball in 1930, guiding OCHS to another spot in the South Jersey championship game. Players like Tom Janneret and Romeo Adelizzi also added to the luster of Ocean City basketball. Bill Kehner became the first player to lead his team in scoring three consecutive years (1939-41). Joe Kennedy repeated the fete (1952-55).

In 1936, Fox became the first Ocean City player to average a double-double. Bringhurst did it again in 1942, Wickes in 1954-55, Hudson in 1956-57 and Fadden in 1957-58. In the 1955-56 season, Thompson became the first Ocean City player to score 40 points in a game. Two years later, Fadden scored 48, a record that stood for 37 years.

There were some very successful swimmers in the early years of the program, before it was disbanded in 1941, including both Fenton and John Carey, Bob Wallace and Swede Drozdov.

OCHS also had successful track and baseball teams and even an occasional tennis team. John Carey won all three throwing events in the state track meet. Jernee was a two-time state track champion. In baseball, Orville Mathis hit .444 and was the No. 1 pitcher to lead the 1959 baseball team to a league title. Larry Harrison was the ace in 1958, also hitting .377 on a championship team. Dave Loder and Joe Kennedy both were the hitting leaders on championship teams. And Bert Avis and Rich Veit were the top hitters in 1952. There were also some OCHS girls sports teams that played limited schedules.

But, if there was one athlete who stood out in the pre-Cape-Atlantic League years, it was Archie Harris. He played four years of football at OCHS (1933-36) – the first two as an end, the last two at fullback. He was a four-year starter in basketball and did his greatest work in track. Harris was strong in all three throwing events but especially in the discus. He had the longest discus throw in the nation as a senior.

The success of Archie Harris did not end with his graduation from high school. He played football in the Big Ten at Indiana University, was a conference all star twice and was an All-American his senior year, finishing among the leaders in the nation in pass receiving. On the Indiana track team, he was a champion in the shot put and set a world record in the discus. Had the 1940 Olympic Games not been cancelled because of World War II, Harris would have been a gold medal favorite.

The specific OCHS records and statistics are not as consistently available in the first half of the 20th Century as they have been more recently. But success always followed the Ocean City teams.

It happened because of Archie Harris. Because of John, Lou and Fenton Carey. Because of Charles and Romeo Adelizzi, Andy Jernee, Joe and Bert Avis, Wayne Hudson, Swede Drozdov, Charlie Bowman, Mike Varano, Walt Buckholtz, Joe Myers, Fran Townsend, Bill Ewing, Bill Morrow and so many others.

This is the first of what we expect to be a series of books highlighting the accomplishments of Ocean City High School athletes, decade by decade. But the young men in this first book are the ones who established the tradition of success and set the goals for all that came after them.

Chapter Twelve

Extra Points

BASKETBALL IN THE 1960S

Season		Coach	Top Scorer	
1968-69	16-7	Jack Boyd	John Huff 14.9	2-1 in NJSIAA
1968	15-6	Dixie Howell	Dave Beyel 14.9	2-1 in NJSIAA
1966-67	15-7	Dixie Howell	John Moore 15.6	1-1 in NJSIAA
1965-66	18-2	Dixie Howell	Rick Howell 18.6	CAL, 2-1 in NJSIAA
1964-65	15-9	Dixie Howell	John Laudenslager 14.9	2-1 in NJSIAA
1963-64	21-4	Dixie Howell	John Cranston 18.8	State, 5-0 in NJSIAA
1962-63	16-7	Dixie Howell	Charlie Baker 15.9	1-1 in NJSIAA
1961-62	19-4	Dixie Howell	Jerry Fadden 17.1	CAL, 2-1 in NJSIAA
1960-61	14-5	Dixie Howell	Gary Satrappe 20.1	CAL, 0-1 in NJSIAA
1959-60	19-2	Dixie Howell	Ken Leary 16.4	CAL, 0-1 in NJSIAA

FOOTBALL IN THE CLASSES OF THE 1960S

Season		Coach	Points (off/def)	
1968	6-2	John Cervino	141-76	
1967	8-1	John Cervino	241-77	CAL champs
1966	3-5-1	John Cervino	119-138	
1965	3-6	John Cervino	100-183	
1964	3-6	Andy Prohaska	97-144	
1963	3-3-2	Andy Prohaska	146-136	
1962	5-3-1	Andy Prohaska	149-65	
1961	2-7	Andy Prohaska	74-176	
1960	3-5-1	Fred Haack	83-120	
1959	6-3	Fred Haack	120-72	

OCHS Football Homecoming Queens

1969	Bonnie Shearer
1968	Gene Beddow
1967	Linda Hunter
1966	Shirley Hashorva
1965	Peggy Gleeson
1964	Linda Guarracino
1963	Pat Gorman

SPORTSPERSONS OF THE YEAR IN THE 1960S
1969   BILL GANS
1968   JOHN CERVINO
1967   FENTON CAREY
1966   CHET WIMBERG
1965   DON PILEGGI
1964   DIXIE HOWELL
1963   BOB FRENCH

SPORTSPERSON OF THE DECADE
1960s   RICHARD B. FOX, JR.

SWIMMING IN THE 1960S

Season		Coach	Captains
1968-69	10-3	Fenton Carey	Tom Bond, Tom Clark
1967-68	6-8	Jim Hutchinson	Don Montagna, Lou Taccarino
1966-67	13-2	Fenton Carey	Ken Penska, Chris Pfaeffli
1965-66	11-5	Fenton Carey	Bill Johnson, Bob Young
1964-65	11-4	Fenton Carey	Ken Ryan
1963-64	10-3	Fenton Carey	Art Carr, Fred Klein
1962-63	12-2	Fenton Carey	Fenton Carey Jr.
1961-62	12-1	Fenton Carey	Mike Hamilton, Hank Schneider
1960-61	9-3	Fenton Carey	John Stull, Ron Van Sant
1959-60	6-4	Fenton Carey	Bob Adams, Bruce Presti

TRACK IN THE 1960S

Season		Coach	CAL
1969	7-4	Ted Klepac	2nd
1968	7-3	Ted Klepac	3rd
1967	6-2	Ted Klepac	1st
1966	6-4	Ted Klepac	2nd
1965	6-4	Ted Klepac	3rd
1964	6-2	Ted Klepac	6th
1963	4-2	Fenton Carey	3rd
1962	3-3	Fenton Carey	4th
1961	4-2	Fenton Carey	2nd
1960	6-1	Fenton Carey	1st

BASEBALL IN THE 1960S

Season		Coach	Top Hitter	
1969	9-8	Fred Haack	John Huff .324	
1968	8-9	Fred Haack	Dave Beyel .363	
1967	9-6	Fred Haack	Frank Kruk .349	
1966	5-9	Fred Haack	Dave Beyel .330	
1965	5-9	Dixie Howell	Larry Masi .322	
1964	12-2	Dixie Howell	Ed McClain .333	CAL champs
1963	12-5	Dixie Howell	Charley Mumford .462	CAL champs
1962	9-6	Dixie Howell	Charley Mumford .460	
1961	11-5	Dixie Howell	Charley Mumford .361	CAL champs
1960	10-3	Dixie Howell	Orville Mathis .364	

Progression of the Career Basketball Scoring Record

1930	Charles Adelizzi (391)
1932	Tom Jeanneret (404)
1937	Dick Fox (495)
1952	Bert Avis (547)
1955	Joe Kennedy (798)
1958	Mike Fadden (829)
1961	Ken Leary (1,063)

Ken Leary – Year by Year

	G	FG	FT-FTA	Points	Ave
1960-61 Senior	20	158	41-77	357	17.9
1959-60 Junior	21	143	59-94	345	16.4
1958-59 Soph	23	147	67-111	361	15.7
Total	**64**	**448**	**167-282**	**1063**	**16.6**

Box Score of 1964 State Final

North Arlington (19-2)	FG	FT-FTA	Pts
Larry Venancio	4	3-4	11
Tom Niemas	3	2-3	8
Tony Cordileone	7	5-8	19
John Boyle	2	0-3	4
Rich Lesson	1	1-3	3
Dan Turnwall	3	0-0	6
	20	**11-21**	**51**

Ocean City (21-4)	FG	FT-FTA	Pts
Bill Haynes	3	1-1	7
John Cranston	7	5-8	19
Barry Banks	4	6-7	14
Randy Fox	9	3-7	21
Ed McClain	5	5-5	15
Bud Swan	0	0-0	0
Craig French	0	0-0	0
John Laudenslager	0	0-0	0
	28	**20-28**	**76**

Score By Periods:

North Arlington	9	10	13	19 –	51
Ocean City	14	14	13	35 –	76

Made in the USA
Columbia, SC
05 June 2017